Markt- und Unternehmensentwicklung Markets and Organisations

Series Editors

Change of institutions, technology and competition drives the interplay of markets and organisations. The scientific series 'Markets and Organisations' addresses a magnitude of related questions, presents theoretic and empirical findings and discusses related concepts and models.

Melanie Oßwald

When Co-Creation Leads to Love

Intersubjectivity in Open Innovation

Springer Gabler

Melanie Oßwald
Friedrich-Alexander-Universität
Erlangen-Nürnberg (FAU)
Nürnberg, Germany

Dissertation Friedrich-Alexander-Universität Erlangen-Nürnberg (FAU), 2024

ISSN 2945-879X ISSN 2945-8803 (electronic)
Markt- und Unternehmensentwicklung Markets and Organisations
ISBN 978-3-658-48889-5 ISBN 978-3-658-48890-1 (eBook)
https://doi.org/10.1007/978-3-658-48890-1

This Springer Gabler imprint is published by the registered company Springer Fachmedien Wiesbaden GmbH, part of Springer Nature.
The registered company address is: Abraham-Lincoln-Str. 46, 65189 Wiesbaden, Germany

"

Imagine you wrote a dissertation on a great topic in open innovation.
You invested years of effort in the underlying studies, elaborately wrote your thesis, love your illustration design, and so you think your creation is awesome.

Will your readers think the same?

Foreword

In an era of rapid technological change and global interconnectedness, open innovation has become a crucial mindset for companies to access a diverse pool of ideas and technologies, speeding up product development and fostering creativity. The challenge for organizations to skillfully select co-creators for their innovation processes has never been more pronounced. Melanie Oßwald addresses one of the most critical and often overlooked aspects of open innovation: how to navigate and mitigate the biases that influence all actors in the innovation process. At the heart of this exploration is the concept of intersubjectivity—the capacity to transcend individual biases and perspectives to reach a shared understanding, a concept that is critical to successfully innovate in the collaborative world.

This book builds on the IKEA Effect, which highlights how co-creation can indeed lead to love: individuals tend to overvalue the contributions they make. Melanie Oßwald delves into the intricacies of evaluation biases that influence the open innovation process. With its comprehensive approach, her book offers valuable insights into the dynamics of co-creation and the crucial role that intersubjectivity plays in fostering effective collaboration. This work offers not only a theoretical understanding of the topic but also practical strategies to foster intersubjectivity in real-world innovation workshops. In doing so, it provides a roadmap for organizations seeking to improve their open innovation practices and ensure that they are selecting the most effective, collaborative partners for their innovation efforts.

As you embark on this exploration of intersubjectivity in open innovation, it is important to recognize that this work is both an invitation and a challenge. It invites us to rethink how we approach collaboration and selection in innovation processes, encouraging a shift from individual-centric evaluations to a more collective, intersubjective framework. At the same time, it challenges us to consider the complexities of human judgment and to adopt new practices that allow us to harness the full potential of collaborative innovation.

The book has been accepted as a doctoral dissertation in 2024 by the School of Business, Economics and Society at the Friedrich-Alexander-Universität Erlangen-Nürnberg (FAU). Its insights and frameworks offer an exciting new frontier for research in open innovation. But more importantly, the book provides actionable strategies for managers, innovators, and researchers alike, making it a must-read for anyone seeking to navigate the complexities of open innovation in today's interconnected world.

Prof. Dr. Kathrin M. Möslein

Abstract

Innovating organizations struggle to select suitable co-creators and their ideas to integrate into their processes. Co-creating market relevance for more than one user is challenging, as co-creators are often individually biased about the value of their contribution. This dissertation is based on one of the best known evaluation biases, the "IKEA Effect: When Labor Leads to Love" (Norton et al., 2012), which provides the inspiration for the dissertation title. Reaching beyond organizational boundaries correspondingly means going beyond an individual evaluation. Intersubjectivity is a key trait for this step beyond individuality. The present work suggests considering intersubjectivity as a concept for efficient open innovation beyond individual evaluation biases.

Four studies aim to create a comprehensive and in-depth understanding of evaluation biases and the concept of intersubjectivity in open innovation. The purpose of the exploratory sequential research design is to gain a holistic understanding of evaluation biases through qualitative research with a narrative literature review and an expert interview study, and then to identify and test new variables on intersubjectivity in several quantitative experiments in the laboratory and in the field.

The data reveal nine overarching topics of evaluation biases emerging from the IKEA effect. These provide guidance on the impact of evaluation biases on open innovation. Evaluation biases can affect all individual roles, not just co-creators, as both as a need and a barrier to the success of innovation co-creation projects. In addition to having varying impact at different stages of open innovation processes, evaluation biases impact differently with the empowerment of co-creators: Creating for oneself or for others is defined as the turning point between positive and negative impacts of evaluation biases. Since evidence repeatedly shows that co-creators cannot learn intersubjectivity, this allocation of evaluation biases is unlikely to change.

Co-creators react irrationally to feedback, according to three experiments in this thesis. Feedback to co-creators leads, on average, to an increase in self-assessment and thus to a feedback-resistance effect. This phenomenon contributes first evidence of a new evaluation bias.

Selecting co-creators on the basis of intersubjectivity as a trait therefore gains even more relevance. The empirical data show that intersubjectivity is a trait in itself, unrelated to creativity. To determine intersubjectivity, two new measurements are presented: the measurement of intersubjectivity between co-creator and user, and the identification of particularly intersubjective co-creators during a workshop. This thesis furthermore proposes strategies to foster intersubjectivity in innovation co-creation workshops, such as a variety of practical balancing methods and relevant co-creator selection criteria. Intersubjectivity could complement existing co-creator types or even form a new overarching selection criterion for co-creators in the future.

Based on these and more insights, implications for open innovation research and for management are derived. These culminate in an inventory of cases in which intersubjectivity is required, and in a working model showing innovating organizations and intermediaries how to implement the concept of intersubjectivity in their innovation co-creation practice. The intersubjectivity working model is complemented by an outlook for future research.

Contents

Abbreviations

AEA	average external assessment
AMA	average mutual assessment
AMAT	average mutual assessment (total)
B2B	business-to-business
cf.	confer
e.g.	exempli gratia (lat.); for example
ESM	Electronic Supplementary Material
et al.	et alii (lat.); and others
etc.	et cetera; and so forth
i.e.	id est (lat.); that is
LERN	Laboratory for Experimental Research Nuremberg
LZE	Leistungszentrum Elektroniksysteme
p.	page
pp.	pages
SA	self-assessment
SAT	self-assessment (total)

List of Figures

List of Tables

1 Introduction: From Assembly Instructions to Shared Outcomes

Supplementary Information The online version contains supplementary material available at https://doi.org/10.1007/978-3-658-48890-1_1.

M. Oßwald, *When Co-Creation Leads to Love*, Markt- und Unternehmensentwicklung Markets and Organisations,
https://doi.org/10.1007/978-3-658-48890-1_1

This introduction section marks the beginning of a research tour towards a more comprehensive and in-depth understanding of the concept of intersubjectivity in innovation co-creation. It sets out the motivation for this dissertation and introduces the reader to the research goals and objectives, before going on to present the structure of this thesis. The introduction concludes with the research design.

1.1 Motivation

"Everyone is an artist—but not everyone is a professional artist." Joseph Beuys[1]

Art is an individual subjective perception that depends heavily on the personal perspective. Artistic creativity traditionally serves an end in itself. Conversely, applied art, such as design, always serves a purpose. Art in its applied form emerged with the advent of industrialization. As a consequence, individual and personal production by the self or by nearby craftspeople was mainly replaced by the anonymous mass production that came with industrialization. The subsequent separation of production from traditional craftsmanship gave rise to the profession of design. Designers were tasked with creating products that would be usable worldwide by as many customers as possible. By becoming empowered to determine what many people use, designers gained a prominent role in product innovation processes. This hierarchical approach, however, led to users becoming detached from the products. In order to fulfill its purpose, design must bridge the distance between the producers and the users, and their different subjective perceptions of the products (Selle, 1997).

How does a designer know that the design is good? That the user likewise thinks it is good? That it fulfills its desired purpose? The answer might be found later in sales figures. Before the success of a design can be measured in sales, however, too much time and too many resources and ideas might be wasted. A designer therefore needs a professionalism that goes beyond the subjective perception of an artist and enables them to create for others. This requires the designer to have a critical distance to their own work and thus the ability to be intersubjective. Designing for someone else beyond your own taste can be hard. In my time as a design student at the Academy of Fine Arts, establishing intersubjectivity was both the toughest, and the most impressive experience that still has a deep impact on me today. I cannot say for myself whether it was a

[1] As one of the most significant action artists of the 20th century, Joseph Beuys is the originator of the "extended definition of art," which implies the idea of a "social sculpture" to redesign society (Ermen, 2010, p. 71).

learning process or whether I simply learned to listen to an intersubjective trait. I have, however, found that it is always worth taking this challenging step, because in the world of design, this trait is considered the key characteristic that makes a designer professional.

Assuming that designers and users are separated as two sides of a coin, there should be some correspondence between the intended use of a design and its actual use. Without a user, design loses its meaning. Yet despite the professional intersubjectivity of designers, this correspondence with users is not always the case. Some aspects still make the success of design at the interface with users unpredictable and therefore pose a commercial risk for innovating organizations that engage designers. Design failures are often caused by a lack of knowledge about tacit and sticky user needs that cannot be captured. In many cases, this is solved by combining the roles, with the designer additionally acting as a potential user for testing. In today's increasingly complex, diversified, and individualized world, down to the level of individual customers (Reichwald & Piller, 2009), this is becoming more and more difficult for designers. Professional design separated from users is less and less able to meet the needs of the masses, despite the best intentions and predictions of traditional market research. With the individualization and democratization of society, the conventional hierarchic imbalance between a single designer and thousands of mass users is becoming problematic (Selle, 1997).

Meanwhile, a new and significant type of creative user has evolved: With users as designers, the do-it-yourself movement has experienced an unprecedented boom in recent years. A considerable part of innovation in a society takes place among users designing products for themselves or at least adapting them to their needs. The immense creative potential of these user innovators exists worldwide (Ogawa & Pongtanalert, 2012). Nowadays, users can do it very professionally for themselves. With the technology and the design software easily available, everyone has the tools they need to feel like a designer and like they are "being an artist," as Joseph Beuys believed (Beuys, 2002). This feeling of being the creator of an innovation can lead to a strong emotional attachment to the creation (Norton et al., 2012). Many innovating organizations have recognized the great potential of the many creative users who can be emotionally engaged through creation. Therefore, organizations are opening up their traditional innovation processes and giving creative users the opportunity to become innovation co-creators (Chesbrough, 2003). Empowering users like this puts a whole new spin on customer centricity (Piller et al., 2011).

Co-creation has many variations. It can, for instance, be conducted with selected or self-selected co-creators for the purpose of generating, testing, or prototyping ideas through focus-group discussions and in workshops. It is a plan that works: The labor that users invest in co-creation leads to a love for the products, a phenomenon known as the IKEA effect (Norton et al., 2012). The love that emerges from co-creation benefits both sides: Users receive products that better fit their needs and make them feel empowered, and organizations gain access to crucial tacit and sticky knowledge and thus better ideas for innovative solutions (Reichwald & Piller, 2009). Moreover, innovative organizations are loved for letting users co-create (Schreier et al., 2013).

If anyone can be a designer now, why are there still professional designers? Beuys additionally said, "… but not everyone is a professional artist" (Beuys, 2002). Professional designers are unquestionably needed for things like complex products or processes and for their intersubjective expertise. Designers progressively take on the role of catalysts of user ideas (Manzini, 2015; Verganti, 2009) and translate user design into mass-producible goods for global markets. It is a logical consequence that designers evolve to become intermediaries between co-creators and innovating organizations. Companies often lack the knowledge and capacity to carry out co-creation projects themselves, so there is a great need for intermediaries (Bessant & Rush, 1995). The economic importance of intermediaries is demonstrated by the increasing collaboration of leading global design agencies with consulting firms. One such example is frog, a design agency that has recently been integrated into Capgemini Invent[2].

I am convinced that co-creation is the future of design. Co-creation with users is the missing link that finally closes the gaps between organizations, designers, and users. That said, co-creation could quickly return to the imbalance where a single user-designed idea faces thousands of other potential users. Intersubjectivity is desperately needed there. This dissertation is intended to be an argument for considering intersubjectivity more in innovation co-creation—after all, it is about design, too.

[2] Frog, an acronym for "Federal Republic of Germany" is a prominent design agency founded in Germany and originally known for its product design, such as for Apple computers: https://www.capgemini.com/about-us/who-we-are/our-brands/frog/.

1.2 Research Objective

Innovating organizations face high demand for novelty from heterogeneous, strongly individualized markets. Moreover, users demand to play a role in designing fitting products, challenging conventional hierarchical and linear innovation processes (Reichwald & Piller, 2009). Opening up innovation processes to users as co-creators expands an organization's capabilities significantly (Prahalad & Ramaswamy, 2000). User knowledge may imply significant economic impact: It may be decisive in avoiding risks and increasing the effectiveness of innovation processes (Bogers et al., 2017; Reichwald & Piller, 2009). Co-creators carry tacit (Cui & Wu, 2015) and sticky need knowledge (von Hippel, 1998) that hired professional designers cannot provide. Moreover, users as co-creators are more emotionally attached to their creations, which can fuel positive perceptions of the product and the innovating organization (Schreier et al., 2013).

This emotional attachment often leads users to develop irrational perceptions of their contribution to the product, typically in the form of overestimating the value of the creation (Ariely, 2008). Such side effects of co-creation are known as evaluation biases (Franke et al., 2010; Norton et al., 2012). According to recent literature, these phenomena mostly have a positive impact on the innovation project (Maier & Baccarella, 2024), such as the emotional bonding of co-creators, which leads to better identification with the co-created products and thus to higher purchase intentions, willingness to pay, customer satisfaction, and recommendations (Schreier et al., 2013). How many of these biases exist and how they are related is still unclear. It is furthermore not known whether there are generally few negative impacts of evaluation biases, or whether they are simply understudied and consequently hardly found in the literature (Maier & Baccarella, 2024). Since evaluation biases are based on a misunderstanding of value, risks arising from misperceptions are likely to be found in open innovation practice (Bogers et al., 2017).

A co-creator's individual evaluation bias impedes their ability to determine the realistic market relevance of their ideas from a managerial perspective. It is uncertain how far an organization's knowledge can be extended by co-creation. Does it add an individual co-creator's capabilities or the capabilities of a whole market? Are co-creators' ideas only meaningful to the co-creators themselves, or do they have broader market relevance that goes beyond one individual? These are crucial questions for exploiting ideas and concepts in innovation co-creation. Figuring this out might result in costly additional market research involving repeated tests or laborious learning cycles. It would be helpful if the co-creators already had an evaluation of their ideas that coincides with a broader range of users or a whole market segment. The shift from an individual perspective to a shared and realistic understanding of the evaluation of, for example, an idea, is known as intersubjectivity (Cooper-White, 2014; Ehkirch & Matsumae, 2024; Shapin, 2017). As mentioned earlier, intersubjectivity is the basis for being able to empathize with others in order to create for them. If the co-creators lack intersubjectivity, it may be more a matter of luck whether a co-created idea is useful to the innovating organization and other users. Identifying co-creators with intersubjective traits at an early stage, or using feedback to train them to produce more realistic evaluations is therefore a promising way for organizations to achieve more efficiency and effectiveness in innovation co-creation projects.

It is therefore relevant to shed light on all facets of biases in innovation co-creation. A comprehensive theoretical explanation of this topic is still lacking. A holistic understanding of the role of evaluation biases may likewise be essential for practitioners. With more knowledge about the phenomena around evaluation and biases, initiators and orchestrators of co-creation could avoid pitfalls and adapt their processes to get the best ideas out of open innovation.

This thesis aims to create a comprehensive and in-depth understanding of evaluation biases and the concept of intersubjectivity in innovation co-creation. The purpose of its exploratory sequential design is, in the first part, to gain a holistic understanding of the phenomenon through qualitative research with a narrative literature review and a corresponding expert interview study. In the second part, new variables on intersubjectivity will be identified and tested in several quantitative experiments in the laboratory and in the field.

1.3 Structure

This dissertation consists of seven chapters and four studies, which are subdivided into sections. Chapter 1 provides the introduction and Chap. 2 illustrates the theoretical foundations. The subsequent studies follow in chaps. 3, 4, 5, and 6, and are then summarized in Chap. 7 with a roundup of the findings and implications. Fig. 1.1 shows the overall structure of the dissertation, as well as the order and arrangement of the chapters.

Chapter 1, "**From assembly instructions to shared outcomes**," introduces the meta research question ("How does intersubjectivity work in open innovation?") and the underlying research. It additionally describes the motivation for this thesis and its research goal and objective. It provides an overview of the structure of this work and closes by presenting the research design, which follows an exploratory sequential mixed methods approach.

Chapter 2 contains the three theoretical **foundations** of this thesis. Innovation co-creation as a form of open innovation is described in the first section, which additionally provides a deeper look at the challenges of selecting co-creators and at the empowerment of co-creators. The second section presents a definition and an overview of evaluation biases. Chapter 2 concludes with a more in-depth introduction to the concept of intersubjectivity.

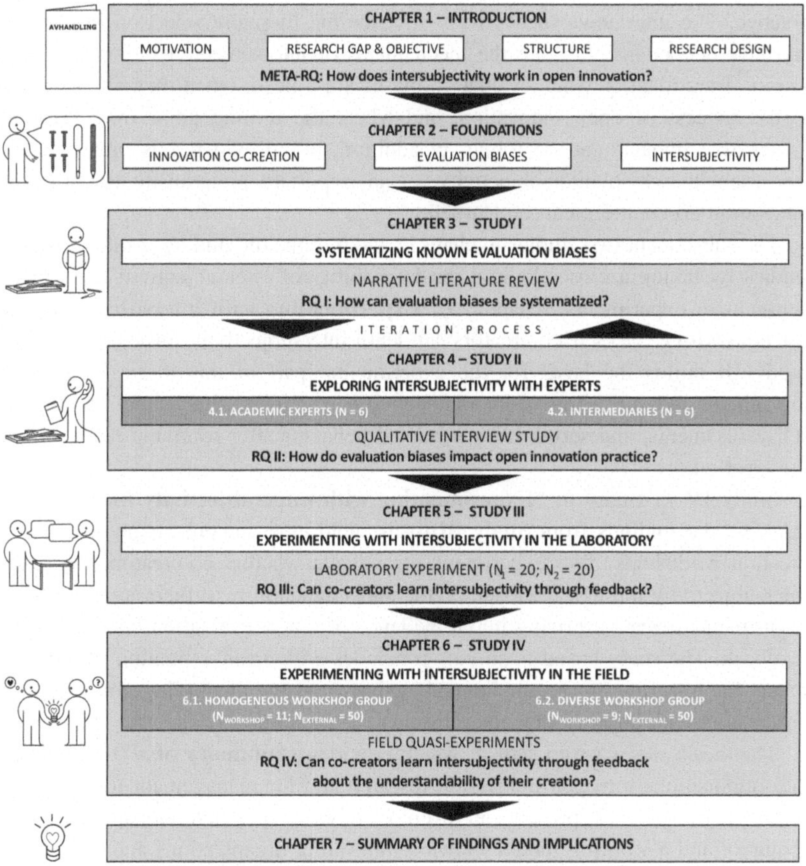

Fig. 1.1 Overall structure of the dissertation. (Author's illustration)

Chapter 3 marks the beginning of the main part, in which four studies build on each other. Study I, "**Systematizing known evaluation biases**," asks how evaluation biases can be systematized. It presents a state-of-the-art literature review of evaluation biases and their impact on innovation co-creation, and condenses overarching topics. Study I is closely linked to Study II through a joint iterative process.

In Chap. 4, "**Exploring intersubjectivity with experts**," 12 experts from academia and practice are asked how evaluation biases impact open innovation practice. The interviews successively advance the literature selection in Study I and give deeper insights into the mechanisms of intersubjectivity in open innovation. They identify when evaluation biases are a need, when they are a barrier to the success of open innovation, and where the turning point from positive to negative impacts can be found. In addition, initial evidence is presented on the extent to which intersubjectivity, as an important prerequisite for efficient innovation co-creation, can be learned.

The subsequent two studies in chaps. 5 and 6 refine the findings of the first two studies by taking a closer look at the learnability of intersubjectivity with three consecutive experiments. Chapter 5, "**Experimenting with intersubjectivity in the laboratory**," asks if co-creators can learn intersubjectivity through feedback. Study III builds the basis for the experimental part of this thesis by exploring suitable measurements of intersubjectivity, examining dimensions for moving self-assessments, and scrutinizing irrational behavior after receiving feedback on the creation.

Study IV in Chap. 6, "**Experimenting with intersubjectivity in the field**," transfers the findings from Study III to the field environment of innovation co-creation workshops. Two experiments investigate whether co-creators can learn intersubjectivity through feedback on the understandability of their creation. Both experiments reveal surprising initial evidence of a new evaluation bias related to feedback. The study-based main part concludes with an investigation of requirements for fostering co-creator intersubjectivity and for identifying and selecting co-creators with an intersubjective trait.

The thesis closes with Chap. 7, which provides a **summary** of all the findings and implications for open innovation research and for management found in the underlying research. It presents an inventory of cases in which intersubjectivity is required, and a working model showing innovating organizations and intermediaries how to implement the concept of intersubjectivity in innovation co-creation practice. It concludes with an outlook for future research.

The investigation in this thesis starts with the IKEA effect, probably the best-known evaluation bias. Inspired by this bias, the chapters are built sequentially, as if assembling a product: from assembly instructions to outcomes shared with the readers. Moreover, icons are used as a stylistic device throughout the thesis as an example of intersubjective design (Urban, 1995). The icons will guide readers through the chapters and fill their bags[3] with key findings.

1.4 Research Design

This section introduces the research design and explains how the research questions are addressed. As a basis, the pragmatic research paradigm is introduced in Sect. 1.4.1. The corresponding exploratory sequential mixed methods approach implies the use of qualitative and quantitative methods in the following studies, which build on each other. These are explained in the subsequent sections.

1.4.1 Research Methodology

Evaluation biases entail different realities simultaneously, which may be balanced by intersubjectivity. This is best expressed in a pragmatic worldview that believes in multiple realities (Cherryholmes, 1992; Creswell & Creswell, 2018). Pragmatism is not content with preconditions. Rather, it consists of actions, situations, and consequences, and is thus application- and solution-oriented (Patton, 2015). Intersubjectivity is not a new topic in design, though its link to open innovation is a new perspective. Pragmatism's openness to different worldviews is an ideal theoretical lens through which to connect different disciplines. This thesis aims to shed light on the full picture of intersubjectivity in open innovation from different angles. To achieve this, both qualitative and quantitative methods are used in an exploratory sequential mixed methods approach. This fairly new methodology focusses on the research question and uses different approaches to understand a topic more holistically (Patton, 2015; Teddlie & Tashakkori, 2009). The results of the different methods can thereby deepen or confirm each other (Rossman & Wilson, 1985). Such data triangulation is well-suited to exploring theory gaps and developing new theory in open innovation (Morse, 1991).

Research on understudied phenomena ideally begins with qualitative approaches (Creswell & Creswell, 2018). This thesis starts with an overarching

[3] The FRAKTA bag helps IKEA customers collect their purchases as they shop. It is an icon in its own right, and one of the most used bags in the world: https://ikeamuseum.com/en/explore/the-story-of-ikea/beloved-bag/.

research question that asks, "**How does intersubjectivity work in open innovation?**". This "how" is furthermore applied in the first two broadly designed qualitative studies to explore different views in a narrative literature review and a qualitative interview study. These are closely connected by an iterative process. This qualitative phase will be used to inductively determine important variables on intersubjectivity to prepare for the follow-up quantitative phase by developing an intervention for the experiments there (Creswell & Creswell, 2018; Morse, 1991).

This thesis is designed to build up successive studies in a sequence. After the qualitative data analysis, the second phase will introduce a transformative change to a quantitative approach, where the insights are deductively refined with two quantitative studies. Initially, a laboratory experiment will be conducted to further specify variables. In line with the pragmatic paradigm, the emphasis of this work is on practitioners. Consequently, two joint field quasi-experiments will ensure the practical relevance of the results.

1.4.2 Narrative Literature Review

Narrative studies are a classical method in qualitative research (Creswell & Creswell, 2018). The exploratory sequential mixed methods approach in this thesis begins with a narrative literature review about evaluation biases. It forms the basis for further exploration of such intersubjectivity phenomena by processing the latest written knowledge on the subject. Evaluation biases such as the IKEA effect are a mature, yet fuzzy topic in many different research disciplines. They are hard to capture with the clearly defined keywords of a systematic literature review. Thus, a narrative literature review has been selected as the method to answer Research Question I: "**How can evaluation biases be systematized?**"

The selected qualitative approach provides up-to-date knowledge about a very specific topic. Context is used for proposing a novel conceptualization of psychological phenomena such as evaluation biases. The focus on patterns and connections among many empirical findings can address questions that are beyond the scope of a single study. It helps identify controversies such as positive and negative impacts of the intersubjectivity mismatch that comes with biases (Baumeister & Leary, 1997). Literature recommends conducting a narrative literature review in unitary, cumulative, and conjunctive stages in a specific order (van de Ven, 1992; van de Ven & Poole, 1995). Findings should be illustrated with visual maps (Langley et al., 2013; van de Ven & Poole, 1995). Juntunen and Lehenkari (2021) provide the application-oriented advice for such explorations using process theory, which fits well with the focus on practical relevance within the pragmatic paradigm.

A unique feature of the literature search and selection is that it was conducted in conjunction with the 12 expert interviews in Study II. This allowed for constant adaptation to new findings until the interviews were completed, leading to a more accurate elaboration of the selected literature and its interrelationships than is otherwise possible with this approach.

1.4.3 Qualitative Interview Study

The narrative approach of the literature review is continued in the qualitative interview study, on which Study II is built. Not all knowledge is written or formulated in searchable literature. Thus, the qualitative interview approach, another classical method (Creswell & Creswell, 2018), was chosen to answer Research Question II: "**How do evaluation biases impact open innovation practice?**" The selected method is particularly well-suited to identifying new categories and to substantiating under-explored areas with individual practice in a social or human problem (Creswell & Poth, 2016; Hammersley, 2013), such as, in this case, the missing aspects for an overall picture of subjectivity in co-creation. To grasp the full picture in the sense of a mixed methodology, the work builds on 12 semi-structured in-depth interviews with experts from academia and practice, i.e., intermediaries for open innovation and user integration. These two groups are considered to have a broad view of co-creation cases with likely reference to the theoretical underpinnings from contrasting viewpoints. This holistic overview and its initial findings mark the end of the first phase of the exploratory sequential mixed methods approach. The thesis then leaves the inductive and qualitative methods, and enters the deductive and quantitative world for further refinement.

1.4.4 Laboratory Experiment

The pragmatic paradigm brings actions and consequences to preconditions, and searches for applications and solutions (Patton, 2015). With that in mind, the laboratory experiment in Study III brings the findings from both studies in Part 1 to life with Research Question III, **"Can co-creators learn intersubjectivity through feedback?"** The present quantitative approach of laboratory experimental methodology has a pretest-posttest control group design with randomization. This is a very common method and offers high internal validity (MacCoun, 2003) for discriminating between alternative theories, such as the indecisive theories of learning intersubjectivity. This approach can find empirical regularities to help extend theory into the new area of intersubjectivity in open innovation (Cassar & Friedman, 2004). The randomization requires less prior knowledge and provides an accurate and statistically unbiased estimate of the effect of an intervention (MacCoun, 2003). The mixed method approach was additionally applied on a small scale within the study design, as there were rarely any suitable variables at hand. The experiment investigated a variety of new measurements and dimensions from creativity research to establish their suitability for the following practical field experiments.

1.4.5 Field Quasi-experiment

The objective of Study IV was to investigate intersubjectivity movements in workshop groups as realistically as possible within the pragmatic paradigm. To complement the previous laboratory experiment, two field quasi-experiments with a one-group pretest-posttest design (O_1-X-O_2) were conducted with different co-creation workshop groups. Research Question IV, **"Can co-creators learn intersubjectivity through feedback about the understandability of their creation?,"** was distilled from the previous findings. The field quasi-experiment method was chosen to gain internal validity in combination with external validity without overly influencing "real life" (Campbell & Stanley, 1966; Grant & Wall, 2009). This method supports generalizability by providing a maximum of realism (Gordon et al., 1986). This approach is particularly suitable for facilitating collaboration with practitioners and using context to explain conflicting findings (Grant & Wall, 2009), such as an irrational impact of feedback on self-assessment.

Since selecting suitable co-creators may be crucial to foster intersubjectivity, quantitative methods are not completely suitable. Choosing specific participants by selecting suitable co-creators does not fit well with the randomization and population of a full quantitative study. Within the pragmatic paradigm, the research approach was therefore adapted to the circumstances by using different methods. In order to gain insights that go beyond the possible significance of very small groups, various experiments were conducted to expand the data. Different group compositions in the field quasi-experiments were compared with each other and with the groups in the laboratory experiment. In addition, the research design was adapted to identify performance groups by considering the Dunning-Kruger test (Schlösser et al., 2013). This was done to deliver further insight into how to determine suitable co-creators with a high degree of intersubjectivity.

The above-described selection of methods for the research design is supplemented by detailed descriptions of their application. These are provided in the corresponding studies in chaps. 3, 4, 5, and 6.

Foundations 2

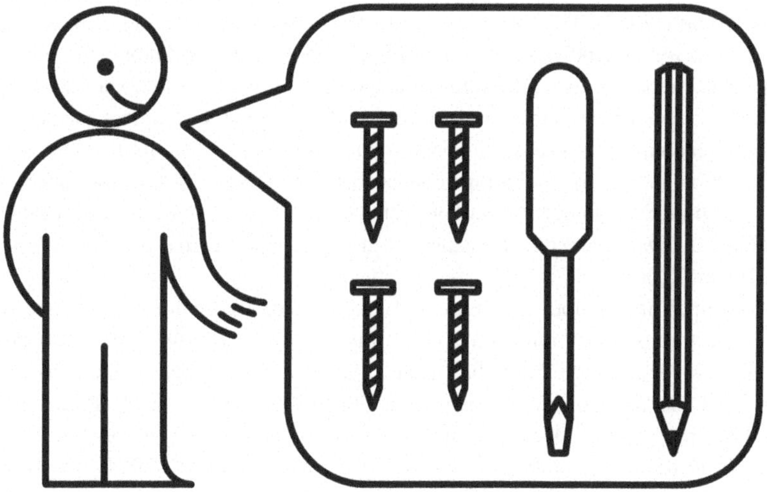

M. Oßwald, *When Co-Creation Leads to Love*, Markt- und Unternehmensentwicklung Markets and Organisations,
https://doi.org/10.1007/978-3-658-48890-1_2

The foundations here in Chap. 2 build the conceptional basis for the research in this thesis. First, innovation co-creation is explained as a form of open innovation that focuses on the creation of new ideas for solutions. The selection of suitable co-creators and their characteristics is therefore relevant, as is the way in which they are empowered. The second section introduces biases, especially evaluation biases, which are then examined in more detail in Chap. 3. The last section introduces intersubjectivity as a shared understanding of evaluation and discusses the role of intersubjectivity in the context of open innovation.

2.1 Innovation Co-creation

Opening up their innovation processes allows organizations to collect rich information about user needs and meeting those needs with solution information (Chesbrough, 2003). The transfer of user ideas into an organization provides better knowledge of crucial sticky (von Hippel, 1994) and tacit knowledge (Cui & Wu, 2015) about an innovation goal that would otherwise not be expressed. This results in a more profitable compatibility between product features and needs. Beyond enabling this market fit, open innovation offers other optimization benefits for organizations, including reduced time-to-market and cost-to-market, as well as an increase in new-to-market (Reichwald & Piller, 2009). To achieve these benefits, innovative organizations need to have an open internal mindset (West & Gallagher, 2006).

The open innovation paradigm finds millions of useful ideas from unobvious others outside an innovating organization. Yet innovative users and ideas often exist outside the box; they cannot be identified in the average of conventional market research (Chesbrough, 2003; Piller et al., 2011; Prahalad & Ramaswamy, 2000). Open innovation integrates these ideas in organizational innovation through an inbound process[1] (Gassmann & Enkel, 2004). Organizations systematically integrating individual users into their innovation processes to create innovation is known as innovation co-creation.

For an innovation co-creation process, typical actors can be defined on different organizational levels: co-creators, the intermediary, and the innovating organization. These actors exist in a specific context relative to each other during

[1] There are two other open-innovation processes for how organizations can deal with external knowledge: An outbound process that externalizes organizational knowledge; and a hybrid form, or coupled process. As these involve different actors and conditions, this dissertation focuses on the inbound process.

the co-creation process, and may appear in other constellations before or after. An overview of innovation co-creation actors in this thesis is given in Fig. 2.1.

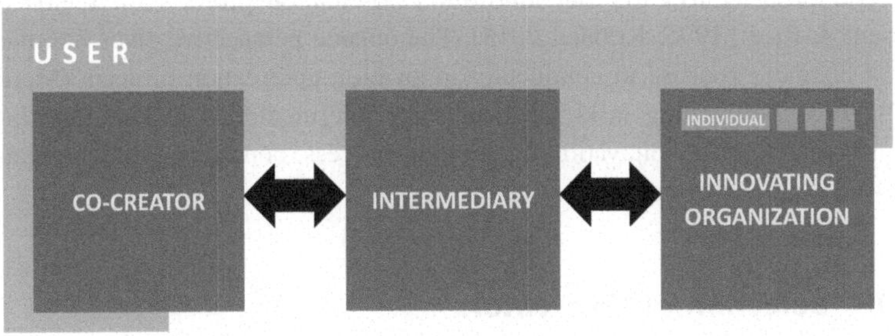

Fig. 2.1 Actors during an innovation co-creation process. (Author's illustration)

These actors fulfill given roles in the innovation co-creation process. Beyond their role as contributors of needs and ideas for possible solutions, users peculiarly have an overarching dual role that can overlap with all other roles. Everyone involved in an innovation co-creation process, be it as a single co-creator or someone who is part of a group, such as an intermediary agency or the innovating organization, is still an individual. All individuals can be potential users of an innovation, no matter what other role they take on (Reichwald & Piller, 2009).

This additionally applies to the innovating organization: Organization theory sees organizations as a social system that consists of different individual roles. In addition to their role within the innovating organization, such as innovation manager, individuals usually hold several other social roles (Katz & Kahn, 1966). Accordingly, in innovation co-creation, the innovating organization may be seen both as a group of individual innovators and as a group of individual, potential users.

Co-creators are systematically and actively involved in the innovation co-creation process, e.g., in workshops. They can be integrated in several ways with different intensity, at different stages of the process (Alam, 2002) and at different locations, e.g., living labs (Greve et al., 2016). In contrast, users are not actively involved in the innovation co-creation process. That said, the possibility of being involved as a co-creator implies that the actor roles of users and co-creators are the most connected. The two have a close relationship because they can easily identify with each other. Therefore, users perceive co-created products and innovating organizations as more attractive than objective product features (Nishikawa et al., 2013; Schreier et al., 2013).

Intermediaries provide co-creation methods and consulting. These individuals may be organized in intermediary agencies and serve as a bridge between co-creators and innovating organizations, as many organizations lack the knowledge and capacity to carry out innovation co-creation projects for themselves (Bessant & Rush, 1995; Krämer, 2015). The outside perspective gives intermediaries a distinct expertise in conducting innovation co-creation projects (Merton, 1972). The coordinating tasks performed by intermediaries include coordinating and managing the innovation co-creation process, conducting the co-creation workshops, and selecting suitable co-creators.

2.1.1 Selection of Co-creators

Selecting suitable co-created ideas for implementation is often difficult and time-consuming for the organizers, as it regularly requires further market research. Not every co-creator input is feasible and immediately fits the innovation goals of the innovating organization. Over time, therefore, the focus has shifted from selecting ideas to selecting co-creators with suitable characteristics that best fit the desired innovation goal. These characteristics are often based on expertise (Oßwald et al., 2019). The selection can additionally be made according to the kind of information expected from the co-creators. Theory distinguishes two information types that can be obtained from knowledge integration through innovation co-creation: need information and solution information. Need information provides evidence about potential needs and requirements. This may help to constrain innovation goals (Bogers et al., 2017). Solution information indicates how these needs and requirements can be satisfied and suggests ways to solve specific problems (Reichwald & Piller, 2009).

Given that any selection of co-creators is biased and usually based on self-reporting only, there is no perfect way to do it. Therefore, the task is often given to intermediaries, who provide better networks and market insights to facilitate the identification of co-creators (Katzy et al., 2013). Open innovation literature indicates suitable selections by identifying five main co-creator types. These are characterized by varying degrees of need or solution information:

- **Lead users** (Huang et al., 2018; Shih et al., 2010; von Hippel, 1986) possess in-depth knowledge of both needs and solutions. Therefore, they are the most sought-after and hardest to find co-creators. Lead users are able to identify needs long before other market participants and they develop solutions with the highest market value potential.

- **Creative consumers** (P. Berthon et al., 2011; P. R. Berthon et al., 2007; Wilson, 2016) modify existing corporate offerings to meet their own unique needs in a do-it-yourself approach. Being very active in sharing their creations, they often provide valuable online content.
- **Emergent nature co-creators** (Hoffman et al., 2010; Vernette & Kidar, 2013) are able to understand the needs of a wider user community early by being imaginative and reflective. They have a high degree of solution information for typical consumer needs.
- **Ordinary users** (Kristensson et al., 2004; T. Schweisfurth, 2016) are the majority of co-creators. They can contribute strong user experience, although less market or technical knowledge.
- **Embedded users** (T. G. Schweisfurth & Herstatt, 2015) are a hybrid form: ordinary users who are simultaneously employees of the innovating company. They are able to combine need information with their advanced technical knowledge.

The highest probability of market success can be obtained with creative consumers, emergent nature co-creators, and lead users (Oßwald et al., 2019). Identifying these is costly, requiring constant monitoring and evaluation across offline and online channels (Hoffman et al., 2010). Finding a way to easily identify suitable co-creator characteristics at an early stage of the collaboration might therefore be of great interest for innovating organizations and intermediaries. This may avoid costly identification efforts and learning cycles, and could consequently increase the probability of suitable solution ideas.

2.1.2 Empowerment of Co-creators

In addition to the different characteristics of the co-creator types, innovation co-creation may be classified according to the way in which co-creators are empowered in a new product development process. This approach is needed to determine the evaluation perspective of the integration. According to an extensive literature review by Maier and Baccarella (2024), this can be categorized in two dimensions: (1) the outcome of the customer or user empowerment activity as a product made for one or for many, (2) customer or user groups according to their involvement in the new product development process, such as participating or just observing.

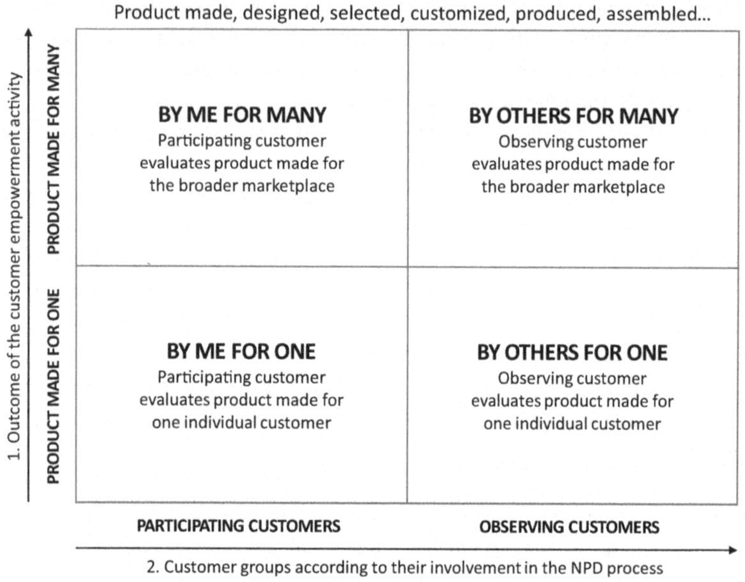

Fig. 2.2 Co-creator empowerment dimensions after Maier and Baccarella (2024)

This results in four "situational natures" as shown in Fig. 2.2, in which the product is made, designed, selected, customized, produced, or assembled. Each of the empowerment dimensions evokes specific psychological and behavioral consequences in the co-creators. These effects have a mostly positive impact on the innovation project, although the positive impact decreases significantly with the distance between co-creators and others:

- **By me for one:** Customers generally react more positively toward customized or self-assembled products with, e.g., higher purchase intentions (C. Moreau et al., 2020) and increased task performance (Kaiser et al., 2016).
- **By me for many:** Customers develop a stronger demand and more mindfulness for the products (Fuchs et al., 2010), although they may be easily disappointed upon rejection of their ideas (Fombelle et al., 2016).
- **By others for many:** Customers mostly react positively to user-designed products with, e.g., higher willingness to pay and recommend (Gebauer et al., 2013).

- **By others for one:** Customers are motivated to express uniqueness (D'Angelo et al., 2019), although they are not willing to pay more for the self-designed products of others due to the equivalent comparison (C. P. Moreau & Herd, 2010).

These co-creator empowerment dimensions are particularly relevant for this thesis because they focus on the different perspectives that a co-creator may face. This makes it possible to systematically classify the intersubjectivity of co-creators in relation to others.

2.2 Evaluation Biases

The review of literature about the consequences of co-creator empowerment shows that involving co-creators triggers psychological and behavioral effects in them. Exchanging experiences plays a crucial role in open innovation (Ramaswamy & Gouillart, 2010). If this collaboration then follows an intrinsic motivation and comes with positive perceptions like appreciation, joy, and competence, the approach achieves its full creative potential (Kristensson et al., 2008; Mochon et al., 2012; K. Roth et al., 2020). Thus, all of this depends on feelings that may result in cognitive biases, which are hard to explain and even more difficult to manage. People tend to act intuitively and irrationally, unlike typical economics approaches, where rationality is the basis for theories, predictions, and recommendations (Ariely, 2008). Behavioral economics addresses this by identifying over 180 cognitive biases (Morrissette, 2021) and trying to offer advice on how to deal with them.

Cognitive biases can basically emerge out of any perception, such as information processing or remembering (Morrissette, 2021). Cognitive biases linked to value, such as evaluation biases, have a specifically economic dimension. This form of bias affects the perception of value, which is the basis of all economic activity. The innovation co-creation approach delivers many beneficial evaluation biases: Even a small amount of effort in open innovation activities, like assembling a product, can trigger love-like feelings in a co-creator (Ariely, 2008). Perhaps the best-known evaluation bias is the IKEA effect (Norton et al., 2012), which was chosen as the initial point of investigation for this thesis. Certainly, everyone who has ever put effort into creating something and later developed a special relationship with the outcome has experienced this phenomenon: People tend to overestimate their own creations and become emotionally attached to the result. This is because overestimating one's own contribution is an everyday evaluation bias (Franke et al., 2010; Norton et al., 2012). Such irrationality on an individual level fuels marketing through customer bonding, better identification with co-created products, higher purchase intentions and willingness to pay, and better customer satisfaction and recommendations (Schreier et al., 2013).

In a nutshell, an evaluation bias creates a certain distance between two value perceptions—between co-creators, users, or the innovating organization. This may not be seen in a negative light at first, because in theory the benefits of this perception mismatch noticeably predominate (Maier & Baccarella, 2024). One may, however, be aware that evaluation biases are based on misunderstandings and can therefore carry risks. These drawbacks of innovation co-creation caused by evaluation biases are rarely pronounced (Elmquist et al., 2009). The more evaluation biases lead to an emotional attachment to the creation, the more dissatisfaction may result in the co-creators from decline of the creation. This may lead to disengagement from and negative word-of-mouth about the innovating organization (Hirschmann, 1970), or even boycott (Richins, 1987) or active resistance and public attacks on organizers by disappointed co-creators (Gebauer et al., 2013).

2.3 Intersubjectivity

> *"How I see, the issue is that basically we create our reality based on language, mostly. Our intersubjective reality. And this is pretty much the whole problem, or where the problem comes into life. Because words and sentences always leave room for interpretation. In design processes, in creative processes, co-creation processes, you have to find a way, to get a... depending on which stage, maybe... minimal or maximum overlap in the intersubjectivity that we experience."*
>
> *(Intermediary Interview 5, Pos. 2)*

This quote from the expert interviews in Study II perfectly sums up what intersubjectivity means in an innovation co-creation context. Individual subjectivity affects co-creation, creative processes in general, how we communicate, and basically how we interact in everyday life: A common understanding of, e.g., an evaluation is the basic prerequisite to make things work together (Shapin, 2017).

The act of swapping an individual perspective in value perception for a shared and realistic understanding of the evaluation of, e.g., an idea, is known in the social sciences as intersubjectivity (Cooper-White, 2014; Ehkirch & Matsumae, 2024; Shapin, 2017). The concept of intersubjectivity was established by Husserl in his Fifth Cartesian Meditation, "Uncovering of the Sphere of Transcendental Being as Monadological Intersubjectivity" (Husserl, 1931). It describes a world constituted jointly and dynamically by individuals (i.e., subjects) working with other individuals (Matsumae & Nagai, 2018). Recent research identifies three interpersonal factors related to intersubjectivity that can be used to quantify intersubjectivity (Ehkirch & Matsumae, 2024): (1) shared understanding (Burford et al., 2013; Cash et al., 2017; Shapin, 2017; Talamo & Pozzi, 2011), (2) empathy (Ho et al., 2011), and (3) boundary objects (Star, 2010). The factor "shared understanding" is most commonly used in literature, so the present thesis focusses on this concept. As a shared understanding, intersubjectivity in innovation co-creation means the perceived legitimacy of an evaluation (Shapin, 2017). Intersubjectivity therefore refers to the distance between two individual subjective perceptions. The smaller this distance is, the greater the intersubjectivity, i.e., the intersubjective level (Ehkirch & Matsumae, 2024). The greater the distance, the greater the perception mismatch, i.e., an evaluation bias. The process of intersubjectivity as a shared understanding is dynamic and involves moving from one's individual subjectivity toward the subjectivity of others, which is referred to as taking a "critical distance" from the work being evaluated (Chong, 2013).

Intersubjectivity as an understanding between individual, subjective perceptions must be distinguished from objectivity. It expresses the relationship between individuals and does not assume a superordinate, objective truth. According to Shapin (2017), the ideal of pure objectivity (Bourdieu, 1986) does not exist. This applies in particular to innovation co-creation: A (co-)creative process is always influenced by taste and is usually irrational and subjective to some extent (Chong, 2013). Art and science are subject to similar problems of value perception, such as conflicts of interest or evidence-based review. Value is a highly subjective matter (Cui & Wu, 2015; von Hippel, 1998). It is not easily transferable, especially when creations are intended to be used by others.

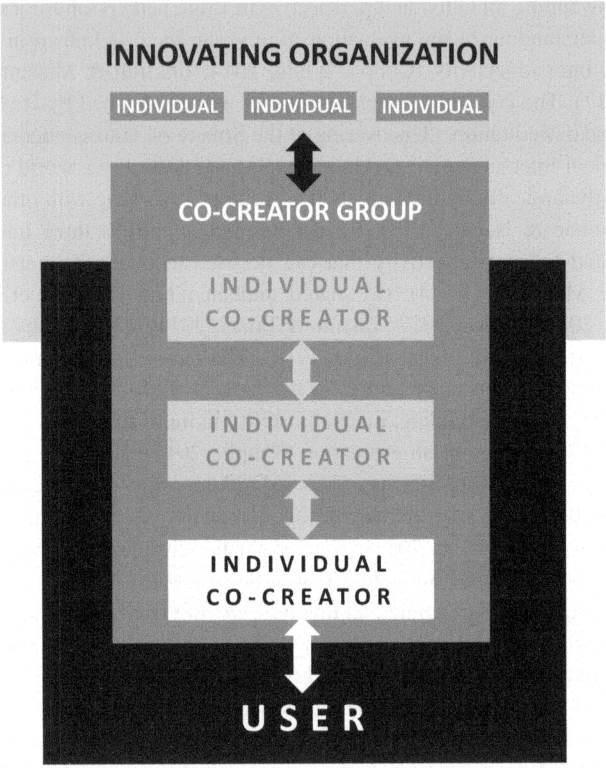

Fig. 2.3 Directions of intersubjectivity. (Author's illustration)

Intersubjectivity between individuals can be established in different directions between the roles in an innovation co-creation process—individuals in the innovating organization, co-creators, and users, as demonstrated in Fig. 2.3. It has already been explored as a shared understanding between co-creators in a group to stimulate fruitful ideas (Amabile, 1983; Cash et al., 2017; Ehkirch & Matsumae, 2024; Matsumae & Nagai, 2018). Intersubjectivity between individuals in innovating organizations and co-creators is already reflected in research on evaluation biases. Yet little is known about intersubjectivity between co-creators and third-party users of the creation. A co-creator might be able to fulfill both roles, so consciously switching between one's own self-estimation perspective and an understanding of other users' perspectives in the sense of taking a critical distance is particularly important in this field. This thesis therefore concentrates on the intersubjectivity between individual co-creators and users who were not involved in the innovation process, i.e., on the empowerment dimension of "by me for many."

Once the direction of intersubjectivity is defined, an intersubjective level can be determined as the difference between individual subjective perceptions of the individual roles in the innovation co-creation process, e.g., between a user and a co-creator. Recent literature suggests measuring the intersubjective level P of co-creation roles in a dynamic context with the equation $P(n + 1) = P(n) + \Delta P$ (Ehkirch & Matsumae, 2024). This approach assumes a more long-term process within a fixed group; its universal applicability in other co-creation settings has not yet been fully explored.

3 Study I: Systematizing Known Evaluation Biases

M. Oßwald, *When Co-Creation Leads to Love*, Markt- und Unternehmensentwicklung Markets and Organisations,
https://doi.org/10.1007/978-3-658-48890-1_3

Study I[1] marks the start of the main part of this thesis. The research journey begins with a structured examination of the complex world of evaluation biases. Starting point is the IKEA effect, one of the most cited and best-known evaluation biases in open innovation. It is still a constant source of inspiration for many other related biases. This provides an ideal basis for the following narrative literature review on evaluation biases.

3.1 Research Objective

Open innovation does not always work as theorized. Bounded rationality provides the foundation for economic theories, predictions, and recommendations, although humans continue to act irrationally (Ariely, 2008)[2]. Human biases and emotions can confound the best open innovation practices through an inherent perception mismatch, so it is crucial for innovating organizations to understand and deal with them. There are over 180 known cognitive biases (Morrissette, 2021). An innovating organization can hardly keep track of them, let alone develop a suitable strategy for handling all of them. Recommendations about which effects are particularly relevant for innovation co-creation and which strategies can be used to address them may therefore be of particular interest to innovating organizations. The first step in such a strategy may be to identify evaluation biases that have a particular impact on innovation co-creation. For example, Michael I. Norton, Daniel Mochon, and Dan Ariely (Ariely, 2008; Norton et al., 2012) found that users are more interested in assembling IKEA storage box kits than in buying them completed, because they overestimate their contribution to the result. Users literally fall in love with their own work during

[1] Study I is based on a previous unpublished conference article (Oßwald & Jonas, 2019) presented and discussed at the 18th Open and User Innovation Conference in Utrecht (Netherlands) and on an unpublished working paper (Oßwald, 2018) at the 2018 research colloquium Innovation and Value Creation in Chemnitz (Germany).

[2] Recently, several of Ariely's publications have come under question because of falsified data. This, however, relates to publications other than those cited in this dissertation. His contribution to the IKEA effect is not affected. For more information, please see https://www.timesofisrael.com/behavioral-researcher-says-he-undoubtedly-made-a-mistake-in-false-data-scandal/.

the assembly process. This mechanism works in a variety of contexts, tangible or intangible. The comparison with falling in love makes strikingly clear how biases work, so the phenomenon is easily understood. Irrational love for one's own creations is not always a disadvantage. On the contrary, some of this emotional attachment can be transferred to the innovating organization as advantages, such as customer bonding, better identification with co-created products, higher purchase intentions and willingness to pay, and better customer satisfaction and recommendations (Schreier et al., 2013). Because these evaluation biases are based on a misunderstanding of value, they do not involve any risks, such as blindness to failure (Thomas & Alluru, 2016).

Norton et al. called the effect they discovered through their storage box kit experiment the "IKEA effect." Several early working versions of the effect were published starting in 2008, and a final publication appeared in 2012 in the *Journal of Consumer Psychology* (Norton et al., 2012). It has been cited 1,537 times to date, which makes it one of the most cited and best-known evaluation biases. This famous, highly interconnected phenomenon has since had an enormous impact on innovation co-creation theory and practice. It provides an ideal basis for a review of evaluation biases.

Defined as an evaluation bias on self-creations, the IKEA effect was first reported in Dan Ariely's 2008 book, *Predictably Irrational* (Ariely, 2008)[3]. According to Norton et al. (2012), the first sources of a bias many years later identified as the IKEA effect can be found in an examination of the willingness to pay for volunteer work in leisure time (Leonard et al., 2003). Another finding from the rise of instant cooking in the 1960s is that labor is likely to be a critical ingredient in recipes (Hubert, 2005). This seems to be an early anticipation of value co-creation (Prahalad & Ramaswamy, 2000) and the IKEA effect. Indeed,

[3] An unrelated effect from the 2000s is also called the IKEA effect and describes a marketing phenomenon, not a bias. This other IKEA effect says that when a new IKEA store opens, customers seem to appear out of nowhere. Established local furniture stores don't seem to suffer significantly from their new strong competitor. This is mostly explained by IKEA's business model, which targets younger and different customers, meaning the effect may just be masking a slow, long-term process. In addition, IKEA stores have much larger catchment areas, with hours of commuting time, than local stores. In addition, they are able to exploit market potential more efficiently, for example through non-essential purchases or cross-selling (Fleischer, 2004; Kayser, 2009).

the IKEA effect has recently been explored in connection with home cooking (Radtke et al., 2019). However, the illustrative legend of its origin in ready-made cake mixes, where the IKEA effect occurs merely through the effort of beating a fresh egg, has since been challenged (Mortimer et al., 2019).

After being perceived as a marketing phenomenon, the IKEA effect as we know it today became an open innovation issue through its close association with the very similar "I designed it myself" effect in mass customization (Franke et al., 2010). These two effects were investigated and published around the same time. Both publications mention each other as a phenomenon that is the reason for the other, a so-called driver. In total, 12 of these drivers are named for the IKEA effect, including the sunk cost effect (Arkes & Blumer, 1985) and the endowment effect (Kahneman et al., 1991). What makes the IKEA effect stand out so much, in addition to its fame and catchiness, is its connection to many similar phenomena in different disciplines such as behavioral economics, marketing, and open innovation. Over a decade after it was published, the IKEA effect remains a constant source of inspiration for identifying countless more evaluation biases. This is where the complexity comes in: A plethora of related effects and biases exist that blur the whole picture. Comprehensive overviews of what biases exist in this field, and whether there is an overarching scheme or theme, are not yet available. Study I therefore raises the following research question:

RQ I: How can evaluation biases be systematized?

3.2 Research Design: Narrative Literature Review

To gain an overview of evaluation biases, a narrative literature review is conducted. The literature recommends organizing a narrative literature review in unitary, cumulative, and conjunctive stages in a specific order (van de Ven, 1992; van de Ven & Poole, 1995) and illustrating them with visual maps (Langley et al., 2013; van de Ven & Poole, 1995). In this regard, the present work follows the suggestions of Juntunen and Lehenkari (2021). They provide application-oriented advice for such explorations using process theory. After this, a review should be designed iteratively in nine steps, containing multiple cumulative written outcomes. The steps are topic selection, definition and research question, development of review protocol, literature search, literature selection, analysis, synthesis, conclusion, and report (Juntunen & Lehenkari, 2021). A literature search can take several forms depending on the objective. Given the clear focus on a distinct evaluation bias in this review, the following types were chosen:

- a search for articles in scholarly journals using specific keywords (Rowley & Slack, 2004);
- a search for publications by authors doing research in the field (Juntunen & Lehenkari, 2021);
- a backward search after citations in the original article (Xiao & Watson, 2019);
- the use of books and other publications to comprehensively describe what is known about the topic (Juntunen & Lehenkari, 2021; Rowley & Slack, 2004).

A unique feature of the literature search and selection in this work is that it was conducted in conjunction with the 12 expert interviews in Study II. This allowed for constant adaptation to new findings until the interviews were completed, leading to a more accurate elaboration of the selected literature and its interrelationships than is otherwise possible with this approach.

3.2.1 Review Procedure

As demonstrated in Fig. 3.1, the narrative literature review started with the topic selection: synthesizing a mature topic (the IKEA effect) and related evaluation biases over a decade after the effect was published. This was followed by the objective definition, a comprehensive description of how evaluation biases are related to each other, and the corresponding research question that asks, "How can evaluation biases be systematized?"

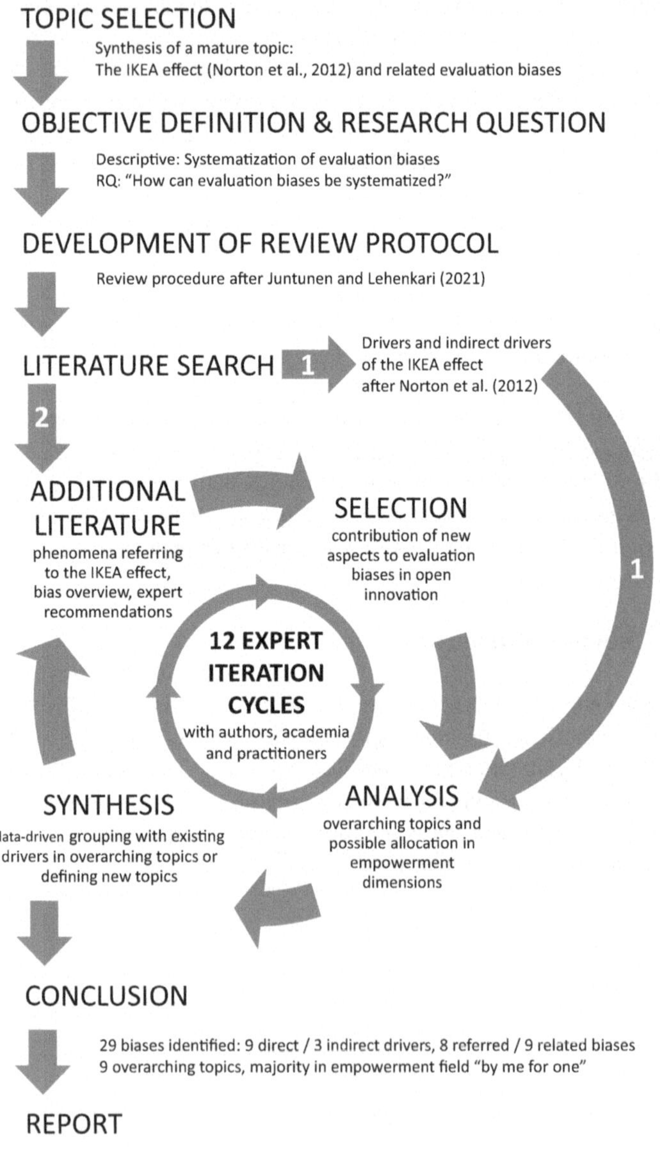

Fig. 3.1 Literature review after van de Ven (1992) and Juntunen and Lehenkari (2021)

From the second iteration cycle on, 12 experts were integrated into the process. They were selected by purposive sampling (Bryman & Bell, 2011) to cover a broad range of input and perspectives. As engaged scholars and intermediaries for open innovation are considered to have a broad overview of co-creation cases, all experts came from academia and practice. A possible close proximity to the topic was balanced by the number of interviews, by careful selection of the experts, and by looking at the topic from contrasting (practical/intermediary) angles. The expert interview process will be explained in detail in Chap. 4. An overview of iterating experts is shown in Table 3.1.

Table 3.1 Overview of iterating experts

CODE	BACKGROUND	POSITION
A1	academic	Professor
A2	academic	Professor
A3	academic	Professor
A4	academic	Professor
A5	academic / independent intermediary	Professor and Director
A6	academic	Professor
I1	independent innovation lab	Managing Director
I2	independent innovation consultant	Design Sprint Coach
I3	innovation consultant	Freelance Innovation Consultant
I4	firm-driven intermediary	Project Manager
I5	independent HR consulting company	Senior HR Specialist
I6	firm-driven intermediary	Global Sales Director

Selection criteria were as follows:

- For academic experts: (1) engagement in open innovation, (2) relevant publications on intersubjectivity and/or evaluation biases in open innovation.
- For intermediary experts: (1) quantity of co-creation projects, (2) diversity in setup (e.g., in-house/boutique/corporate consulting or local/global; broad/niche), (3) proximity to scholarly work.

The experts were provided with the current version of the literature review and explicitly asked about their opinion on the literature selection, its synthesis, and their recommendations for missing topics or biases. Upon completion of the 12 iteration cycles, a conclusion was drawn and the present report was written.

3.2.2 Data Collection and Analysis

The literature analyzed in this study was collected by using two approaches for literature research: one fixed and one iterative for finding additional literature. The fixed literature search emerged from a backwards search of the drivers mentioned in the original IKEA effect article (Norton et al., 2012). These are divided into nine direct drivers, which are cited in the original article, and three indirect drivers, whose corresponding biases are mentioned as an influence but are not directly cited.

Identifying and collecting additional literature was performed in an iterative process and consists of two types: referred biases that directly refer to the IKEA effect, and related biases. The initial search for referred biases started with a literature search for the term "IKEA effect" on EBSCO Host[4] and Google Scholar[5]. The results were then selected based on their contribution of new aspects to the topic and their number of citations. Repetitions of the known effect procedures in other fields or mere overviews were rejected. This was underpinned by the identification of possibly related biases from the book *Predictably Irrational* (Ariely, 2008) and a comprehensive cognitive bias collection (Morrissette, 2021). In this way, the iterative process with the experts started with a first version of the additional literature of six referred and six related evaluation biases.

During the iterative process, the experts added a number of new biases to the additional literature, especially in the related biases category. They additionally rejected some biases that they thought did not fit the list. After the completion of the iterative process, the literature search with the term "IKEA effect" on EBSCO Host and Google Scholar was repeated to ensure that recent publications of referred biases were captured. This added one more referred bias, which was published in 2023: the buy-in effect (Dykstra et al., 2023). Finally, the data collection was completed with eight referred biases and nine related biases (i.e., with a total of 29 evaluation biases), and subjected to further analysis.

To facilitate the data analysis, the found literature was condensed into a brief description of the respective evaluation bias as shown in Table 3.2. These descriptions have been written in the style of known bias collections (Morrissette, 2021) in short sentences in the first person. As far as possible, they follow the same pattern in order to emphasize the differences and similarities. Comparing and contrasting then identified nine overarching topics. Some of these overarching topics coincide or even contain each other, which is why some biases are mentioned more than once.

---

[4] https://search.ebscohost.com

[5] https://scholar.google.com

Table 3.2 Overview of evaluation biases found in literature

THE "IKEA EFFECT": WHEN LABOR LEADS TO LOVE (NORTON, MOCHON & ARIELY, 2012) "I place higher value on things that I have invested effort into."		**OVERARCHING TOPICS**
"Liking through effort" (Aronson & Mills, 1959)	The more effort I invest in my possession, the more I like it.	**BIASED OWNERSHIP**
Endowment effect (Kahnemann et al., 1991)	I demand more to give up something than I would pay to acquire it.	
Ownership bias (Ariely, 2008)	The more work I put into something, the more I feel ownership for it.	
"Possession and ownership" (Furby, 1991)	Possession gives me control and a sense of self.	
"To have is to be" (Dittmar, 1992)	The things I own are part of my self-identity.	
(Reverse) trophy effect (Bühren & Pleßner, 2013)	If I win with it, I place higher value in it.	
"Possession and ownership" (Furby, 1991)	Possession gives me control and a sense of self.	**FEELINGS OF EFFECTANCE**
"To have is to be" (Dittmar, 1992)	The things I own are part of my self-identity.	
"Liking through effort" (Aronson & Mills, 1959)	The more effort I invest in my possession, the more I like it.	**INVESTED EFFORT**
"To have is to be" (Dittmar, 1992)	The things I own are part of my self-identity.	
Endowment effect (Kahnemann et al., 1991)	I demand more to give up something than I would pay to acquire it.	
Ownership bias (Ariely, 2008)	The more work I put into something, the more I feel ownership for it.	
Buy-in effect (Dykstra et al., 2023)	The more effort I invest in something, the more I use it.	
"Escalation of commitment" (Staw, 1981)	I give more commitment, the more effort I invested.	
Escalation bias (Biyalogorski et al., 2006)	I misapply positive beliefs and make more effort when faced with new negative information.	

(continued)

Table 3.2 (continued)

Sunk cost effect (Arkes & Blumer, 1985)	I invest more in things that have cost me something, even if I face negative outcomes.	
"Overcommitment in management" (Schmidt & Calantone, 1998)	I am more committed the more innovative the idea is, regardless of its feasibility.	
"Construction enhances product value" (Walasek et al., 2017)	I place higher value on self-constructed things when I own them.	
Self-creation effect (Brunneder & Dholakia, 2018)	When I create something for myself, I use it more mindfully.	**SUSTAINABIL-ITY**
Buy-in effect (Dykstra et al., 2023)	The more effort I invest in something, the more I use it.	
"Construction enhances product value" (Walasek et al., 2017)	I place higher value on self-constructed things when I own them.	**INCORPORA-TION INTO THE SELF**
"Identification through self-production" (Atakan et al., 2014)	How I identify with my creation depends on the creation stage I was involved in.	
"Extension of self-identity" (Marsh et al., 2018)	Things I partially created myself become a part of my self-identity.	
"Feelings of competence" (Mochon et al., 2012)	Creating something makes me feel competent and raises my self-esteem.	
Customization bias (Franke et al., 2009)	If I can express my preferences better, I place higher value on the result.	
I-designed-it-myself effect (Franke et al., 2010)	I place higher value on things I partially created myself.	
Customization bias (Franke et al., 2009)	If I can express my preferences better, I place higher value on the result.	**CONTROL**
I-designed-it-myself effect (Franke et al., 2010)	I place higher value on things I partially created myself.	
"Constrained creativity" (Dahl & Moreau, 2007)	When I create something, I enjoy it more if the task is controllable.	
"Control over outcomes" (Bandura, 1977)	When I create it for myself, I have full control over it.	

(continued)

Table 3.2 (continued)

Handmade effect (Fuchs et al., 2015)	I place higher value on things that others have invested effort in.	**VALUE TRANSFER**
Innovation effect of user design (Schreier et al., 2013)	I see companies as more innovative if they involve users like me.	
Self-serving bias (Miller & Ross, 1975)	My failures are situational, but my successes are my responsibility.	**EGOCENTRISM**
Dunning-Kruger effect (Kruger & Dunning, 1999)	The less expertise I have, the more confident I am in my judgement.	
Overconfidence effect (Pallier et al., 2002)	My confidence in my judgment is greater than its accuracy.	
Better-than-average effect (Alicke & Govorun, 2005)	I evaluate myself more favorably than an average peer.	
Not-invented-here syndrome (Katz & Allen, 1982)	I evaluate my own work more highly than new ideas of others.	
Novelty paradox (Boudreau et al., 2012)	The more I am an expert, the more critical I am of others' new work in the field.	
"Disastrous consequences of the IKEA effect" (Thomas & Alluru, 2016)	Placing higher value on my creations makes me blind to their failure.	
Escalation bias (Biyalogorski et al., 2006)	I misapply positive beliefs and make more effort when faced with new negative information.	
Sunk cost effect (Arkes & Blumer, 1985)	I invest more in things that have cost me something, even if I face negative outcomes.	
"Overcommitment in management" (Schmidt & Calantone, 1998)	I am more committed the more innovative the idea is, regardless of its feasibility.	
Escalation bias (Biyalogorski et al., 2006)	I misapply positive beliefs and make more effort when faced with new negative information.	**NEGATIVE IMPACT**
Sunk cost effect (Arkes & Blumer, 1985)	I invest more in things that have cost me something, even if I face negative outcomes.	

(continued)

Table 3.2 (continued)

"Overcommitment in management" (Schmidt & Calantone, 1998)	I am more committed the more innovative the idea is, regardless of its feasibility.	
Not-invented-here syndrome (Katz & Allen, 1982)	I evaluate my own work higher than new ideas of others.	
Novelty paradox (Boudreau et al., 2012)	The more I am an expert, the more critical I am of others' new work in the field.	
"Disastrous consequences of the IKEA effect" (Thomas & Alluru, 2016)	Placing higher value on my creations makes me blind to their failure.	

During data analysis, the results of the literature search were additionally investigated after their possible allocation to the empowerment dimensions following Maier and Baccarella (2024) to gain more information about the perception mismatch of the respective bias. This information was then synthesized by grouping the results into overarching topics. New overarching topics were added as they emerged. All of this was then transferred to a visual map. The results are presented in the following sections of the findings.

3.3 Findings

Following the review procedure described above, a total of 29 biases related to the IKEA effect were identified: nine direct drivers and three indirect drivers, eight referred biases and nine related biases, shown in Fig. 3.2. They can be grouped into nine overarching topics. Of those that were assignable to the empowerment dimensions, most were assigned to "by me for one." The following chapters will present these findings in detail. Designated effects are listed by their name, while descriptions of phenomena without specific names are represented by brief abridgments in quotes.

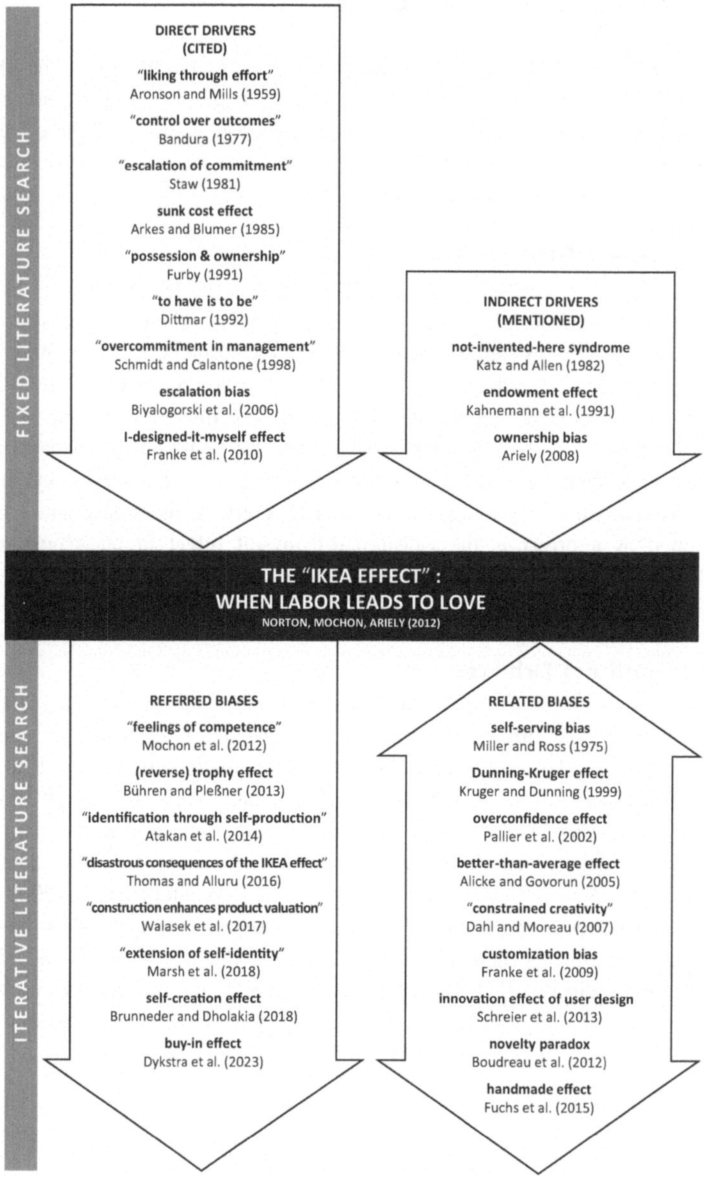

Fig. 3.2 Literature search findings. (Author's illustration)

3.3.1 Drivers of the IKEA Effect

The drivers of the IKEA effect come from the main publication "The IKEA Effect: When Labor Leads to Love" by Norton et al. (2012). They are either mentioned directly as an underlying bias and therefore a driver of the effect, or they are mentioned as influencing biases, which form the indirect drivers in the literature selection. These findings are presented in detail in the following.

3.3.1.1 Direct Drivers

The main article by Norton et al. (2012) found that the IKEA effect is largely driven by several underlying, long-established psychological mechanisms. The article names the biases "liking through effort" (Aronson & Mills, 1959), "control over outcomes" (Bandura, 1977), "escalation of commitment" (Staw, 1981), the sunk cost effect (Arkes & Blumer, 1985), "possession and ownership" (Furby, 1991), "to have is to be" (Dittmar, 1993), "overcommitment in management" (Schmidt & Calantone, 1998), and the escalation bias (Biyalogorsky et al., 2006a). At the time of publication of the IKEA effect, the sole contemporary effect cited as a driver is the I-designed-it-myself effect in mass customization (Franke et al., 2010). As described above, the history and scope of both phenomena is closely linked.

3.3.1.2 Indirect Drivers

Interestingly, the Norton article mentions two other influencing biases of the IKEA effect without direct reference: the not-invented-here syndrome and the endowment effect. The not-invented-here syndrome as investigated by Katz and Allen (1982) is therefore represented in the literature selection as an indirect driver. The reference to the endowment effect is rather unusual, as the main article explicitly distinguishes the IKEA effect from the endowment effect. The first mention of the IKEA effect in literature by Norton's co-author Ariely (2008) and by other researchers (e.g., Shmueli et al., 2012) identify the ownership bias and the endowment effect, which was described by Kahnemann, Knetsch, and Thaler (1991) as the main driver of the IKEA effect. Thus, the indirect drivers in the literature search findings of this study were completed with the ownership bias (Ariely, 2008) and the endowment effect (Kahneman et al., 1991).

3.3.2 Additional Literature

The selection of additional literature about biases related to the IKEA effect emerges from the literature search and the expert iteration cycles in the review process. The publications from the literature search were selected for their contribution of new aspects to evaluation biases in open innovation and can be divided in two categories: referred biases, which directly refer to the IKEA effect and may be seen as a kind of evolutionary history of the main publication; and related biases, which arose predominantly from the experts' suggestions and were discussed further in the subsequent iteration cycles up to the final status presented in detail in the following.

3.3.2.1 Referred Biases

The literature search found that several connatural biases directly follow and refer to the IKEA effect in the following years, and add new aspects to the picture of evaluation biases. This literature review investigated "feelings of competence" (Mochon et al., 2012), the (reverse) trophy effect (Bühren & Pleßner, 2014), "identification through self-production" (Atakan et al., 2014), "disastrous consequences of the IKEA effect" (Thomas & Alluru, 2016), "construction enhances product valuation" (Walasek et al., 2017), "extension of self-identity" (Marsh et al., 2018), the self-creation effect (Brunneder & Dholakia, 2018), and the buy-in effect (Dykstra et al., 2023).

3.3.2.2 Related Biases

The iterative process with experts identified a number of biases from open innovation literature that can be seen as closely related to the IKEA effect, as they describe comparable or partial aspects of the phenomenon. These biases are the self-serving bias (Miller & Ross, 1975), the Dunning-Kruger effect (Kruger & Dunning, 1999), the overconfidence effect (Pallier et al., 2002), the better-than-average effect (Alicke & Govorun, 2005), "constrained creativity" (Dahl & Moreau, 2007), the customization bias (Franke et al., 2009), the innovation effect of user design (Schreier et al., 2013), the novelty paradox (Boudreau et al., 2012), and the handmade effect (Fuchs et al., 2015).

3.3.3 Allocation to Empowerment Dimensions

The found publications on drivers and biases were first investigated for their possible allocation to the empowerment dimensions after Maier and Baccarella

(2024). The texts were searched for indications of whether a particular empowerment perspective was used to describe the bias, and were then tagged accordingly. This was done to understand the perspective from which they were written and thus their possible relation to intersubjectivity in open innovation. Although evaluation biases originate from a lack of intersubjectivity, most (16) of the 29 phenomena could not be assigned to any field of the empowerment dimensions because the corresponding publications did not focus on one distinct perspective. Of the 13 that were assignable to the empowerment dimensions, nine were assigned to the field "by me for one," as presented in Fig. 3.3.

Fig. 3.3 Allocation of literature search findings in empowerment dimensions after Maier and Baccarella (2024)

These were "escalation of commitment" (Staw, 1981), "constrained creativity" (Dahl & Moreau, 2007), the customization bias (Franke et al., 2009), the I-designed-it-myself effect (Franke, Schreier, Kaiser, 2010), "feelings of competence" (Mochon et al., 2012), "construction enhances product value" (Walasek et al., 2017), "extension of self-identity" (Marsh et al., 2018), the self-creation effect (Brunneder & Dholakia, 2018), and the buy-in effect (Dykstra et al., 2023).

Three phenomena—the novelty paradox (Boudreau et al., 2012), the innovation effect of user design (Schreier et al., 2012), and the handmade effect (Fuchs et al., 2015)—could be assigned to the field "by others for many." One phenomenon—"identification through self-production" (Atakan et al., 2014)—was assigned to the field "by me for many." No identified publication could be assigned to the field "by others for one."

3.3.4 Overarching Topics

To facilitate the classification into overarching topics, the literature was condensed into a brief description of the respective bias, as shown in the data analysis in Table 3.2. Comparing and contrasting the short descriptions identified nine overarching topics: *biased ownership, feelings of effectance, invested effort, sustainability, incorporation into the self, control, value transfer, egocentrism,* and *negative impact.* Some of these main topics coincide or even contain each other.

The allocation of evaluation biases to overarching topics is given as follows:

- **Biased ownership**: "liking through effort" (Aronson & Mills, 1959), endowment effect (Kahneman et al., 1991), ownership bias (Ariely, 2008), "possession and ownership" (Furby, 1991), "to have is to be" (Dittmar, 1993), (reverse) trophy effect (Bühren & Pleßner, 2014).

  Biased ownership additionally contains *feelings of effectance.*
- **Feelings of effectance:** "possession and ownership" (Furby, 1991), "to have is to be" (Dittmar, 1993).
- **Invested effort:** "liking through effort" (Aronson & Mills, 1959), "to have is to be" (Dittmar, 1993), endowment effect (Kahneman et al., 1991), ownership bias (Ariely, 2008), buy-in effect (Dykstra et al., 2023), "escalation of commitment" (Staw, 1981), escalation bias (Biyalogorski et al., 2006), sunk cost effect (Arkes & Blumer, 1985), "overcommitment in management" (Schmidt & Calantone, 1998), "construction enhances product value" (Walasek et al., 2017).

- **Sustainability:** buy-in effect (Dykstra et al., 2023), self-creation effect (Brunneder & Dholakia, 2018).
- **Incorporation into the self**: "construction enhances product value" (Walasek et al., 2017), "identification through self-production" (Atakan et al., 2014), "extension of self-identity" (Marsh et al., 2018), "feelings of competence" (Mochon et al., 2012), customization bias (Franke et al., 2009), I-designed-it-myself effect (Franke et al., 2010).
- **Control**: customization bias (Franke et al., 2009), I-designed-it-myself effect (Franke et al., 2010), "constrained creativity" (Dahl & Moreau, 2007),"control over outcomes" (Bandura, 1977).
- **Value transfer:** handmade effect (Fuchs et al., 2015), innovation effect of user design (Schreier et al., 2013).
- **Egocentrism**: self-serving bias (Miller & Ross, 1975), Dunning-Kruger effect (Kruger & Dunning, 1999), overconfidence effect (Pallier et al., 2002), better-than-average effect (Alicke & Govorun, 2005), not-invented-here syndrome (Katz & Allen, 1982), novelty paradox (Boudreau et al., 2012), "disastrous consequences of the IKEA effect" (Thomas & Alluru, 2016), escalation bias (Biyalogorski et al., 2006), sunk cost effect (Arkes & Blumer, 1985), "overcommitment in management" (Schmidt & Calantone, 1998).

  Egocentrism fully contains the topic *negative impact.*
- **Negative impact:** escalation bias (Biyalogorski et al., 2006), sunk cost effect (Arkes & Blumer, 1985), "overcommitment in management" (Schmidt & Calantone, 1998), not-invented-here syndrome (Katz & Allen, 1982), novelty paradox (Boudreau et al., 2012), "disastrous consequences of the IKEA effect" (Thomas & Alluru, 2016).

These findings, together with the allocation of evaluation biases in empowerment dimensions, are synthesized in a visual map in the following.

3.3.5 Visual Map

Taking together the allocation to the empowerment dimensions and the overarching topics of the found fixed and iterative literature, this work comes to the following synthesis shown as a visual map in Fig. 3.4. Each of the overarching topics and how they relate to one another are elaborated on and explained in this section. Topics that contain other topics in their entirety are considered together.

Biased ownership and feelings of effectance

The first and oldest explanation of the IKEA effect refers to variations of *biased ownership* (Ariely, 2008), in particular through the endowment effect (Kahneman et al., 1991), which generates feelings of ownership, such as liking, through special invested efforts (Aronson & Mills, 1959) in the creative process. These feelings of ownership can be reinforced—positively and negatively—in a competitive situation to the (reverse) trophy effect (Bühren & Pleßner, 2014). Norton et al. (2012) note that biased ownership additionally implies the topic of *feelings of effectance* through the social psychology of—in this case, assumed—possessions (Dittmar, 1993) and personal definitions of "mine" (Furby, 1991).

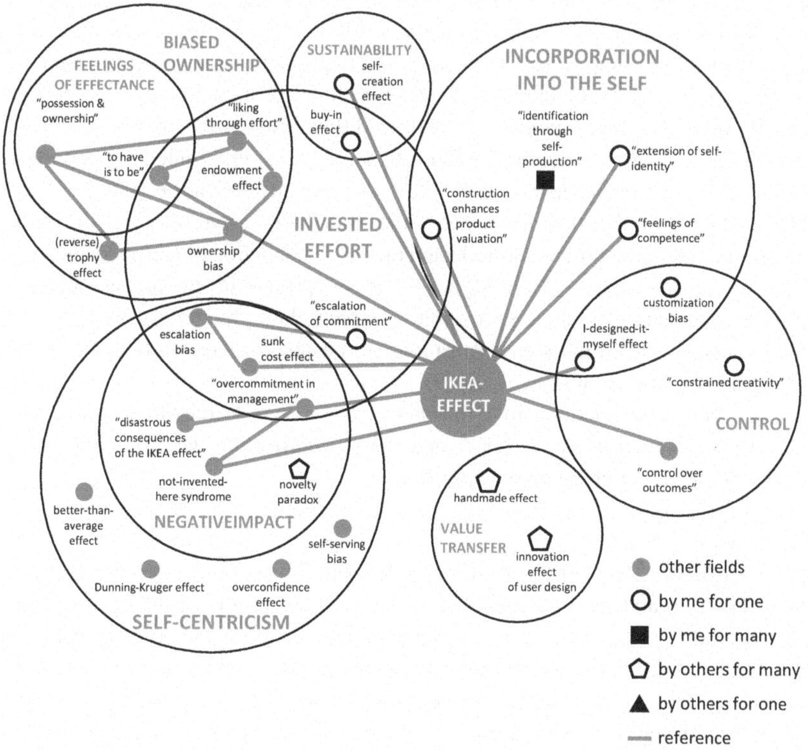

Fig. 3.4 Map of the IKEA effect and related evaluation biases. (Author's illustration)

Incorporation into the self

Definitions of ownership may become so strong that they lead to the *incorporation of the creation into the self*. This topic represents a more recent stream of literature to emerge from the IKEA effect. There, the empowerment dimensions are remarkably concentrated on the perspective "by me for one," with the exception of one phenomenon. Research found that self-assembled objects are incorporated into the self (Atakan et al., 2014), especially when their creator owns the product (Walasek et al., 2017). This adds a new twist to the traditional ownership and effort-based approaches, as it complements the aspect of extending self-identity by contributing to products or services (Marsh et al., 2018). Incorporation does not work without effort during creation, or without progress and enjoyment during a co-creation process in an open innovation setting (Franke & Schreier, 2010). As well as leading to a higher valuation of the result, the IKEA effect can additionally serve as proof of competence. Therefore, it is important to always leave room for the status thinking of the creators. Threatening the self-confidence of the creator actually increases the propensity to create and thus restores the creator's sense of competence (Mochon et al., 2012). This phenomenon is represented in open innovation with the I-designed-it-myself effect in mass customization (Franke et al., 2010), which describes the importance of the co-creators' awareness of their role as the originators of the product, as reflected in, e.g., the labeling of self-made beanies with "my selfmade boshi" from Myboshi[6]. It is important for the higher valuation of the results that the co-creators are able to express their preferences properly, and that the tasks, e.g., in mass customization, are designed accordingly to evoke the customization bias (Franke et al., 2009).

With their close relationship to the balance between task freedom and task control, the I-designed-it-myself effect and the customization bias are additionally located in the overarching topic *control.*

Control

Control is a small but powerful overarching topic, involving the conflict between the difficulty (and thus valuation) and the realistic solvability of the creative task. Norton et al. (2012) describe task completion as crucial for the emergence of the IKEA effect. Further research on connatural effects states that the negative effects of the IKEA effect, such as subjective over-requirement in the design process, depend on the task design (Shmueli et al., 2012). Control can therefore be understood as control over the integration process itself (Dahl & Moreau, 2007), especially over the level of difficulty and thus successful completion of the task (Franke et al., 2009,

[6] https://www.myboshi.net

2010). It may likewise mean perceived control over the outcomes (Bandura, 1977), for example through the integration of co-creators into a development process.

Value transfer

That the perceived value of creations is transferable is slightly different from other overarching topics. Although this is a related phenomenon to the IKEA effect, it is not directly referred to. It comes from authors who have already contributed many articles on the subject. The contained effects describe self-creations and the affection for them. The creator and the observing appreciator are not the same in these cases. This means that the higher valuation comes with the product, so that, in addition to the transfer of knowledge during the innovation process, the valuation of the invested effort is transferred, too. The handmade effect (Fuchs et al., 2015a) uses this mechanism to explain why "made with love" products are so attractive to their users, e.g., on platforms like Etsy[7]. This is surpassed only by the innovation effect of user design (Schreier et al., 2013), where co-created products directly increase consumers' perceptions of the producer's innovative ability. This is the case with co-created cosmetic products for drugstores, for instance[8].

Invested effort

Invested effort is the largest and most controversial overarching topic. With its broad overlap with other fields, the work invested in creations can be seen as a superordinate theme, even affecting both the positive and negative impacts of the IKEA effect. Five other topics relate to *invested effort*: *biased ownership* through assumed possession, *feelings of effectance* and therefore endowment (Ariely, 2008; Aronson & Mills, 1959; Dittmar, 1993; Kahneman et al., 1991), *sustainability* due to increased use (Dykstra et al., 2023), the *incorporation into the self* by constructing an item (Walasek et al., 2017), and *self-centrism* with *negative impacts* such as commitment escalation (Arkes & Blumer, 1985; Biyalogorsky et al., 2006a; Staw, 1981) to disastrous consequences from management biases, partially induced by the not-invented-here syndrome (Katz & Allen, 1982; Schmidt & Calantone, 1998; Thomas & Alluru, 2016). The invested effort invoked in the subtitle "When Labor Leads to Love" is evident as a major theme, as all of these contained phenomena are referenced in the original publication of the IKEA effect or directly refer to it.

---

[7] https://www.etsy.com

[8] https://www.wuv.de/Archiv/Social-Media-Seife-dm-lässt-Duschgel-auf-Facebook-entwickeln

Egocentrism and negative impact

A perception mismatch plays a role in all topics around the IKEA effect, and a certain amount is always the reason for a bias. Some of the evaluation biases evolving in this literature selection are particularly related to *egocentrism* because of their origin in self-focus. Half of the phenomena in this topic were explicit suggestions made by the experts for completing the picture around the IKEA effect, as described in Chap. 4.These are well-known effects that result from misjudgments (Kruger & Dunning, 1999; Pallier et al., 2002) and explicitly poor evaluations of others (Alicke & Govorun, 2005; Miller & Ross, 1975). It can go as far as judging others' new ideas in one's own field as particularly bad (Boudreau et al., 2012). This points to the overarching topic of *negative impact*, which is entirely in the realm of *egocentrism.* A complete rejection of others' ideas is likewise located in this field (R. Katz & Allen, 1982). Just like real love, the IKEA effect tends to create a kind of subjective blindness that comes from thinking contingently and not being open to outside influences. Norton et al. (2012) initially state for themselves that the over-evaluation of own creations can lead to negative outcomes through the IKEA effect: They see sunk cost effects (Arkes & Blumer, 1985; Staw, 1981) as a reason for escalating commitment to projects that are in fact failing.

In this context, the *invested effort* again plays a decisive role, though this time it is negative. This occurs in organizations as well as on an individual level and can have disastrous consequences on new product development, e.g., in companies (Thomas & Alluru, 2016) when managers fall into overcommitment (Schmidt & Calantone, 1998) for their own amateurish and therefore potentially bad ideas.

Sustainability

The most recent literature stream emerging from the IKEA effect is that of *sustainability*. The contained buy-in effect (Dykstra et al., 2023) and the self-creation effect (Brunneder & Dholakia, 2018) are both located in the perspective "by me for one" in the empowerment dimensions and are good examples of how the IKEA effect has inspired many other phenomena. Invested effort or higher valuation leads to more and mindful use. This desirable benefit of the IKEA effect is a fairly recent finding in the literature. It can be expected that more will follow.

3.4 Discussion

When looking at the IKEA effect as one of the most heavily researched evaluation biases, it can be said that this form of bias has many more aspects than invested effort. This narrative literature review investigated evaluation biases on the basis of the IKEA effect to gain a comprehensive overview of what biases exist in this field and how they can be systematized. The result is 29 interconnected evaluation biases. These biases are categorized into nine direct and three indirect drivers, as well as eight referred and nine related biases. A further catalyzation leads to nine overarching topics of evaluation bias. These topics demonstrate how evaluation biases are discussed in related research fields in scholarly work. The iterative cycles with experts additionally provide a first glimpse of the topic from an academic and practitioner perspective, which will be deepened in the next chapter.

This study reveals that evaluation biases have both positive and negative impacts on innovation co-creation. So far, open innovation theory has focused on the benefits of biases, with little evidence of when negative effects occur. Knowing where the risks of these biases lie would be beneficial. The categorization of evaluation biases identified in this narrative literature review provides initial indications that the impact of evaluation biases varies with the empowerment dimensions of co-creators. These findings are further discussed from a research and a managerial perspective in the following sections.

3.4.1 From a Research Perspective

There are nine overarching topics of evaluation biases

The nine overarching topics identified around the IKEA effect contribute to theory by providing a comprehensive systematization of evaluation biases. The overarching topics are: *biased ownership, feelings of effectance, invested effort, sustainability, incorporation into the self, control, value transfer, egocentrism,* and *negative impact*. These go beyond the previously known reasons for the occurrence of these biases, such as invested effort or biased ownership, and provide orientation in a previously complex research field.

Evaluation biases have positive and negative impacts

Since the impact of evaluation biases differs among the co-creator empowerment dimensions, a turning point may exist where positive individual subjectivity becomes negative. This aspect requires further investigation, as many of the biases analyzed are not originally from the field of open innovation research, even though they strongly influence on it. This is especially true for the topics *egocentrism* and *negative impact*, where there is little direct reference to open innovation in the present literature. Regarding this, the experts made some recommendations about effects not yet considered in relation to the IKEA effect, which describe two sides of perception mismatch. For example, although the Dunning-Kruger effect is mostly known for overconfidence at low levels of expertise, it moreover states that accurate self-estimation arises with increasing expertise and that even underestimation can arise with high expertise (Kruger & Dunning, 1999). This might be an interesting approach for further investigation into the two sides of intersubjectivity in open innovation.

3.4.2 From a Managerial Perspective

Evaluation biases depend on more factors than invested effort or biased ownership

Study I describes how biases can have a varying impact on innovation co-creation. Systematizing the nine overarching themes of evaluation biases provides practitioners with clarity and guidance on which biases they could pay particular attention to when engaging co-creators and where potential pitfalls lie.

Impact of evaluation biases depends on empowerment dimension of co-creators

Even if many of the phenomena identified do not originate from the field of open innovation, they still influence innovation co-creation. The visual map can give a first indication of the context in which benefits or disadvantages of evaluation biases occur. Positive impact, such as supporting self-image and sustainability through more mindful use, are closely linked to a "by me for one" empowerment dimension, where it is only about the individual who is actively involved. This heavily self-centered perspective in users may not always have the same positive impact on the innovating organization. The topic *negative impact* contains several examples of how positive commitment can turn into toxic behavior through egocentrism with a high perception mismatch. Nevertheless, there seem to be certain cases of value transfer in which a perception mismatch with a high valuation can be transferred to others. These cases are all located in a different field of the empowerment dimensions: that of "by others for many."

3.4.3 Summary of Findings

In summary, the narrative literature review defined nine overarching topics of evaluation biases: *biased ownership, feelings of effectance, invested effort, sustainability, incorporation into the self, control, value transfer, egocentrism,* and *negative impact*. These provide guidance in a complex research field and go beyond the previously known reasons for these biases, such as invested effort or biased ownership. The broad identification of evaluation biases and their associated topics on the basis of the IKEA effect shows that their impact can vary. Evaluation biases have positive and negative impacts on innovation co-creation. This study provides first indications for boundaries between these different impacts: The impact of evaluation biases varies with the empowerment dimensions of co-creators. Positive impact is linked to the highly individual "by me for one" empowerment dimension. However, the benefits of the innovating organization can fall out of focus and lead to a negative impact through egocentrism and a resulting a perception mismatch. Nevertheless, in the "by others for many" empowerment dimension, there are certain cases where a perception mismatch can be transferred to others. Future research could further explore the boundaries between the positive and negative impacts of evaluation biases.

YOUR ITEMS FROM STUDY I

- There are nine overarching topics of evaluation biases: *Biased ownership, feelings of effectance, invested effort, sustainability, incorporation into the self, control, value transfer, egocentrism* and *negative impact*
- Evaluation biases provide positive and negative impact on innovation co-creation
- The impact of evaluation biases varies with empowerment dimensions of co-creators

4 Study II: Exploring Intersubjectivity with Experts

Supplementary Information The online version contains supplementary material available at https://doi.org/10.1007/978-3-658-48890-1_4.

M. Oßwald, *When Co-Creation Leads to Love*, Markt- und Unternehmensentwicklung Markets and Organisations,
https://doi.org/10.1007/978-3-658-48890-1_4

The last chapter examined how evaluation biases are related to each other through different research fields and topics in literature. Now Study II[1] complements these findings with in-depth interviews with the academic and intermediary experts who were involved in the iterative process of the narrative literature review. While the last chapter looked at evaluation biases in different research fields, this chapter focuses on evaluation biases and intersubjectivity, particularly from an open innovation perspective.

4.1 Research Objective

Evaluation biases impact innovation co-creation positively and negatively, with a probable turning point in between, as the last chapter found. It is essential for innovating organizations to gain an overview so they can understand and handle evaluation biases. Suitable strategies need to be found to address both sides of evaluation biases in a beneficial way. This can avoid innovation risks and failures due to misunderstandings. The initial step for this was the identification of evaluation biases and their overarching topics in Study I. Although the identified evaluation biases have a major impact on open innovation practice, not all of them emerged from this research field, especially in the overarching topics *egocentrism* and *negative impact*. In fact, it turns out that—with the exception of the field "by me for one"—the effects in the co-creator empowerment dimensions (Maier & Baccarella, 2024) have hardly been researched at all. A distinct exploration of this topic is still lacking. This chapter complements Study I by looking at and extending its findings from an open innovation perspective. The goal is to examine the role of evaluation biases in open innovation practice by investigating the benefits and risks of co-creators' subjectivity, as well as methods for dealing with biased co-creators.

Study II aims to identify how open innovation practice can balance the positive and negative impacts of evaluation biases. This leads to the following research question:

RQ II: How do evaluation biases impact open innovation practice?

[1] Study II is based on a previous, unpublished conference article (Oßwald, Jonas, & Möslein, 2023) that was presented and discussed at the 24th CINet Conference in Linz (Austria).

4.2 Research Design: Expert Interview Study

For the purpose of investigating this research question, a qualitative approach was chosen to identify new categories and substantiate underexplored areas with individual practice in a social or human problem. In order to gain a deeper understanding of evaluation biases, this study conducted 12 semi-structured in-depth interviews with experts from academia and practice, i.e., intermediaries for open innovation and user integration. Academic experts were chosen to establish a link from evaluation biases to open innovation research that is often missing in recent literature. Intermediaries provide a diversified, external view of co-creation methods and insights that innovating organizations usually do not have for themselves (Bessant & Rush, 1995; Krämer, 2015; Merton, 1972). It is assumed that these two groups have a broad overview of the cases of co-creation and are likely to refer to the theoretical underpinnings from contrasting points of view.

For the selection of interviewees, purposive sampling was used (Bryman & Bell, 2011) to cover a broad range of input and perspectives, and to mitigate biases. Possible close proximity, especially among some academic experts who have discovered relevant evaluation biases, was balanced by the number of interviews, by careful selection of the interviewees, and by looking at the topic from a contrasting (practical/intermediary) view. An overview is given in Table 4.1.

Selection criteria were as follows:

- For academic experts: (1) engagement in open innovation, (2) relevant publications on intersubjectivity and/or evaluation biases in open innovation.
- For intermediary experts: (1) quantity of co-creation projects, (2) diversity in setup (e.g., in-house/boutique/corporate consulting or local/global; broad/niche), (3) proximity to scholarly work.

Table 4.1 Overview of expert interviews

PARTICIPANT	BACKGROUND	POSITION	DURATION
A1	academic	Professor	0:23:01
A2	academic	Professor	0:19:13
A3	academic	Professor	0:38:08
A4	academic	Professor	0:27:01

(continued)

Table 4.1 (continued)

PARTICIPANT	BACKGROUND	POSITION	DURATION
A5	academic / independent intermediary	Professor and Director	0:29:08
A6	academic	Professor	0:21:16
I1	independent intermediary / innovation lab	Managing Director	1:13:33
I2	independent intermediary / innovation consultant	Business Designer and Design Sprint Coach	1:01:01
I3	independent intermediary / innovation consultant	Freelance Innovation Consultant	1:05:09
I4	firm-driven intermediary / digital consulting	Project Manager	0:55:02
I5	independent intermediary / HR consulting company	Senior HR Specialist	0:59:26
I6	firm-driven intermediary	Head of Strategic Business Field and Global Sales Director	0:35:30

Intermediary interviews were held with another researcher to allow data triangulation for a deeper understanding of possible links to open innovation theory (Morse, 1991). For the interviewed experts' comfort, they could choose whether to do the interview in English or German (Creswell & Poth, 2016). Three interviews with academic experts (A1, A2, A3) were conducted in person. The following elaborated interviews with academic experts (A4, A5, A6) were held shortly afterwards via telephone. The intermediary experts were interviewed via a video conferencing platform.

The interview goals were two-fold: First, the current literature review findings from Study I were presented to stimulate feedback on evaluation biases in scholarly work and on their comprehensiveness. Second, the interviews aimed to open a discussion around specific evaluation biases and enhance the picture of academic findings with experience of evaluation biases in practice. The interview guide (see Appendix B in the Electronic Supplementary Material) reflects the best-known evaluation biases in four general questions (Ariely, 2008; Franke et al., 2010; Norton et al., 2012), as well as theory on intersubjectivity (Cooper-White, 2014; Ehkirch & Matsumae, 2024; Shapin, 2017) and critical distance (Chong, 2013).

The interviews lasted on average 42.5 minutes, ranging from 19 to 73 minutes. At the beginning of the interview, each expert gave oral consent for being recorded. The interviewees were all guaranteed anonymity.

4.3 Data Collection and Analysis

To enable early reflection on the data, the audio files of the interviews were transcribed and then revised by the researcher shortly after each interview. The transcript files were then transferred to MaxQDA software[2]. Expert I6 sent a mind map and written statements to complement their interview. These were cross-referenced to help place the following coding in a broader context. During coding, the data were kept in its original language to stay as close to the sense of the original statements as possible (Temple & Young, 2004).

The data were first structured in a mind map with regard to a later possible data structure following the recommendations of Gioia et al. (2013). This was done using an open, inductive approach (Miles et al., 2013) with regard to the research question. The four topics in the interview guide (subjectivity, balance, critical distance, and lack of intersubjectivity) served as an initial orientation for the codes. During data analysis, the codes were accompanied by the respective exemplifying quotes. The search for similarities and differences in the codes identified 24 first-order concepts. A further search for nascent concepts distilled seven second-order themes. From these themes, three dimensions were further aggregated to form a full data structure as illustrated in Fig. 4.1.

To illustrate the results, verbatim exemplifying quotes are provided together with the results in the following sections. If needed, these quotes were translated into English using DeepL software[3]. To verify the correct transition of meaning, forward-backward translation was used, along with an additional revision by the researcher.

---

[2] https://www.maxqda.com

[3] https://www.deepl.com

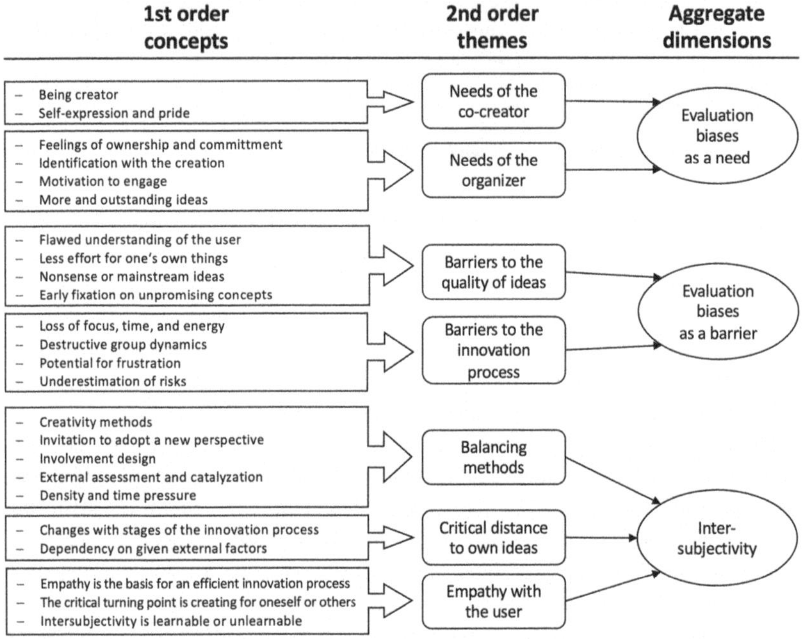

Fig. 4.1 Data structure of the interview study after Gioia et al. (2013)

4.4 Findings

From the data analysis, it can be concluded that evaluation biases have a broad impact on open innovation practice in multiple ways. Evaluation biases can (1) play the role of either a need or (2) a barrier in co-creation. It is derived that (3) balancing both sides with intersubjectivity is the basis for an efficient innovation process. This section presents the findings and discusses how these dimensions are interrelated. For transparency and to summarize aspects, the findings will use citations from interviewees in tables (Patton, 2015).

4.4.1 Evaluation Biases as a Need

The above-described data analysis indicated that evaluation biases can be seen as a need from two sides: the needs of the co-creator and the needs of the organizer. The needs of co-creators are *being creator* and *self-expression and pride.*

Co-creators have a human desire to create and to feel empowered, which may provide immense potential for innovation. Co-creation can give them the desired opportunity to express themselves and feel pride. The needs of the organizer include *feelings of ownership and commitment, identification with the creation, motivation to engage,* and *more and outstanding ideas.* This study brings forward that organizers may equally benefit from evaluation biases: Practitioner experience finds that they lead to stronger feelings of ownership, more identification with the creation, and more motivation to engage—all factors that finally lead to more and outstanding ideas.

4.4.1.1 Needs of the Co-creator

Being creator

This interview study derives that the subjective need to create and thereby feel empowered is deeply rooted in human beings. Interviewees confirmed that this is one of the basic prerequisites for open innovation. User innovation cannot be neglected. The potential of creative amateurs following a booming do-it-yourself trend (Ogawa & Piller, 2006; Ogawa & Pongtanalert, 2012) may deliver competitive advantages (Chesbrough, 2003) when integrating them into open innovation practice. An estimated 3–6% of the world's population is active as a customer or user innovator, investing more effort and money than their economies officially spend on research and development (Ogawa & Pongtanalert, 2012).

Self-expression and pride

Co-creating is a valid method of self-expression and for feeling pride. Even though overconfidence and a corresponding perception mismatch can be very strong, the interviewed experts did not currently see this as a problem. Data analysis nevertheless shows that this factor should not be ignored, since negative consequences may likewise arise from intense evaluation biases, e.g., if other individuals do not agree with the creation. Theory finds more and more amateurs expressing themselves and their needs by creating their individual products or modifying existing products. They identify through self-production (Atakan et al., 2014) and it extends their self-identity (Marsh et al., 2018). Accordingly, Franke et al. (2010) recommend that co-creators should have the opportunity to show their pride, e.g., in social media. This is already practice in some innovation contexts, as the experts described.

4.4.1.2 Needs of the Organizer

Feelings of ownership and commitment

It was found that evaluation biases are a reliable way to bind co-creators to the innovating organizer. Even just touching a product is enough to increase the value associated with it. This is known in theory as the endowment effect (Kahneman et al., 1991). With even a small amount effort, such as assembling the product, this overevaluation may transition into love-like feelings and blatant overestimation of one's own contribution, as similarly reflected in theory (Ariely, 2008). These forms of biases give a sense of personal competence or control, and a connection between perceived possession and the self (Furby, 1991). The analysis of the expert interviews showed that this additionally helps motivate and maintain the perceived individual ownership of an idea across groups and time periods in a co-creation process, giving it a form of flexibility.

Identification with the creation

Beyond ownership, identification with the creation is another important need for the innovating organization, and co-creators can fulfill this through their evaluation biases. Data show that believing in one's own creation and imagining oneself as the originator of a potentially great innovation helps build a relationship with the organizer—who in turn has the possibility to bond the co-creator with this bias. According to literature, the co-creators' emotional bonding and thus valuation results in better identification with co-created products, higher purchase intentions, willingness to pay, and better customer satisfaction and recommendations (Schreier et al., 2013).

Motivation to engage

Just as creation is a basic human need, this investigation found that the innovating organization needs the co-creators' individual evaluation biases to motivate their participation. If creative amateurs do not engage, their powerful potential for competitive advantage (Chesbrough, 2011) cannot be integrated into the innovation process. The data analysis found that evaluation biases can be used to energize and motivate co-creators to continually put more effort into their creation and to achieve better results. This invested effort can lead to more love-like feelings (Franke et al., 2010; Norton et al., 2012), which then induce perseverance for overcoming risks or other challenges during the further innovation process.

More and outstanding ideas

According to the data analysis, the evaluation biases of the co-creators have the great advantage of generating more and outstanding ideas than when a group works on only one idea. This is because the individual perceptions of the co-creators during a workshop seem to put them in a competitive situation, which makes them more productive. In addition, the interview study found that these ideas are usually of higher quality and more unconventional because they are not smoothed out by the mainstream. It is important to ensure that these outstanding ideas do not get lost in group dynamics.

Together with the three preceding concepts, the data showed the following chain of effects: evaluation biases lead to more feelings of ownership, which leads to more identification with the creation, which leads to even more motivation to engage, which leads to more and outstanding ideas (Table 4.2).

Table 4.2 Exemplifying quotes on "evaluation biases as a need"

EVALUATION BIASES AS A NEED	
Needs of the co-creator	
Being creator	It is (…) a deep-seated human need to create something. (A1)
Self-expression and pride	If I like my self-designed T-shirt, no one else has to like it, so it's the subjectivity that counts. (…) In extreme cases, this can perhaps lead to megalomania, but that in itself is not a problem, but rather the consequences of it. (A1)
	(…) I transfer my needs, what I think is good, what I like into the design and express myself through it. (A3)
	That you have the idea (…) and somehow also get attention as a result, especially in social media. Such effects, and that there (is) a form of "Proud of My Product" or some kind of pride. (I4)
Needs of the organizer	
Feelings of ownership and commitment	It kind of starts in my head, but it becomes a group idea for a group concept. And then there are other groups on an equal footing that give feedback on it. (…) you would probably continue to work with this group in the later course of the workshop (…), do further iterations. So that this ownership is there again and enables them to pursue this idea further. (I3)
	If people do something themselves, they own it (…) And ownership that reflects on motivation, reflects creativity, reflects commitment, reflects basically part of the culture in which a team, an organization is set in, and in which individuals have a certain freedom to navigate in. (I5)

(continued)

Table 4.2 (continued)

EVALUATION BIASES AS A NEED	
Identification with the creation	I believe that the type of emotional drive (…) in ideal case it's very positive. Obviously, you are biased by definition, if you are emotionally attached, but I believe when we are dealing with innovation, feelings and intuitive gut feelings are not necessarily bad for at least some part of the team members. (I6)
	He identifies with the solution. He imagines that somehow it can be in one big shot. He was the creator, the idea generator, so to speak. And you have to play with that to a certain extent. For us, as a quasi-consulting agency, it is essential to have someone on the client side who believes in this and who then builds a relationship with us. (I3)
Motivation to engage	This effect is very important for the team later on to continuously being motivated to work on their projects. (I2)
	If I think something is very valuable, I might try harder, and if I think it's not very valuable to others, then of course I won't try as hard to spread it because I don't see the point. (A3)
	You need a little bit of emotion and a little bit of "I'm burning for this now," otherwise you're not going to get through all the hurdles. (A5)
More and outstanding ideas	Either you have a very mature group that can actually resolve conflict, because conflicts are good, right? They actually help you to increase A) the quality of your work, of your projects, and B) if you are good at this, you can also learn from it, because every conflict is a chance. (I5)
	Especially in such creativity workshops, when it comes to innovation, subjectivity is actually very important. Because otherwise we remain in the mainstream. (…) You actually have to be careful in the workshop that these individual opinions are not sacrificed, for some group dynamic reasons, or just to follow the crowd, or not to stand out too much, or whatever. (A6)
	It's OK to have different opinions, especially in the early stage, because it can bring more aspects for the potential solution. (I6)

4.4.2 Evaluation Biases as a Barrier

The expert interview study reveals that evaluation biases, on the contrary, may still become a barrier to the success of co-creation—regarding the quality of ideas as well as the innovation process. Barriers to the quality of ideas are *flawed understanding of user, less effort for one's own things, nonsense or mainstream ideas,* and *early fixation on unpromising concepts.* Besides leading to a flawed understanding of the user due to self-overestimation effects, evaluation biases can cause a general lack of effort, which may lead to a lower quality of ideas and early fixation on unpromising concepts. The following barriers to the innovation process were identified: *loss of focus, time and energy; destructive group dynamics; potential for frustration;* and *underestimation of risks.* Evaluation biases may disturb innovation processes through a loss of focus, often caused by destructive group dynamics in workshops. They may contain a higher potential for frustration and therefore angry reactions and an underestimation of risks.

4.4.2.1 Barriers to the Quality of Ideas

Flawed understanding of the user
Evaluation biases have many advantages. Too much individual thinking does, however, have disadvantages. First and foremost, the data analysis shows that there may be a flawed understanding of the users. In most cases, co-creators are at the same time potential users of the solution, and this naturally tempts them to make false assumptions about others, as reported from practice. The reason for this may lie in the self-overestimation of one's own creation, as described in phenomena such as biased ownership through the endowment effect (Kahneman et al., 1991), the IKEA effect (Norton et al., 2012), and the I-designed-it-myself effect (Franke et al., 2010).

Less effort for one's own things
Surprisingly, evaluation biases can furthermore lead to a general lack of effort. Concentrating too much on oneself may make co-creators apathetic, idle, and closed off. This is the opposite of what one would naturally assume, given that being creative is supposed to be a human need, as described above. In practice, some people seem content with getting what they want and have no ambition to go beyond their individuality. This trait prevents the idea from being available to others. Overly strong evaluation biases could be the reason why people close themselves off like this. It may be likewise due to miscommunication about the co-creation goals, such as who the idea is for, or how to share the idea. It could also be a problem with

co-creator selection. These cases might additionally contain an inappropriate co-creation task, and the share of labor described in the theory could therefore be reaching its limits (Reichwald & Piller, 2009).

Nonsense or mainstream ideas

While evaluation biases can lead to individual unconventional ideas, they can have the opposite effect, too, as the data reveal in a new contribution to recent theory. The aforementioned lack of effort may cause co-creators to become idle and with this less creative. They then tend not to think outside the box and are likely to deliver nonsense or mainstream ideas. Data analysis attributes this to professional experience, which can lead to more efficiency orientation and can hinder creativity. Moreover, it was revealed that this bias can affect all individual roles: Intermediaries pointed out that they themselves struggle not to get too involved into the co-creation project and to maintain a critical distance so they can still fulfil their role as facilitator and enabler of outstanding ideas.

Early fixation on unpromising concepts

Co-creator apathy caused by overly strong evaluation biases may lead people to fixate on a solution too quickly. Cited reasons for this behavior included an overly efficiency-oriented education. Co-creators seem to like what they already have, and they can obviously lack the critical distance to see that their preferred solution is not promising. People often just see the invested effort, which leads to a stronger commitment. In the theory, this bias is known as escalated commitment (Staw, 1981). The sunk cost effect (Arkes & Blumer, 1985) may similarly stand behind this phenomenon. Both biases describe the tendency to continue an activity when money, effort, or time have been invested, even though one often suspects that the concept will not succeed, a phenomenon correspondingly found in this study.

4.4.2.2 Barriers to the Innovation Process

Loss of focus, time, and energy

A much-discussed matter in this empirical study is that falling in love with one's own creation (Norton et al., 2012) is a gift, though one that can simultaneously make you blind to your surroundings. Data show that self-centeredness can lead co-creators to forget, during the innovation process, who they are creating for and what the problem really is. The loss of focus due to evaluation biases can cost time, energy, motivation, and money. The data additionally revealed a new aspect: that intermediaries can be subject to evaluation biases, too. This can happen when they are tempted to think too individually and thus confuse their role as moderator with that of a user. The resulting lack of guidance can then reinforce the negative impact of evaluation biases, e.g., in a workshop group.

Destructive group dynamics

It was found that conflicts are inevitable when many subjectively charged ideas emerge. This is not inherently negative and may even have a positive impact on the outcomes by presenting more ideas for how to solve one problem. Especially in workshops, though, this can lead to destructive group dynamics. Not every group can handle this in a constructive way. Evaluation biases can lead co-creators to fiercely defend their own opinion. Egocentric, dominant personalities with a "need for nonconformism" may negatively influence the entire innovation project. To achieve useful results and avoid wasting time, it is even more important to assemble or moderate co-creation groups appropriately regarding the personalities of the participants.

Potential for frustration

Stimulating evaluation biases in co-creators can induce an even higher potential for frustration and may evoke dissatisfaction and negative reactions towards the innovating organization. Since evaluation biases are necessary for initial motivation, there will always be some degree of self-overestimation. The higher the level of self-overestimation, the lower the mood can fall when it becomes clear just how big the difference in the perception mismatch was. This potential for frustration is a particular danger in innovation projects where only one solution is implemented in the end. All other failing ideas can disappoint those who created them, as described in the theory (Gebauer et al., 2013; Hirschmann, 1970; Richins, 1987).

Underestimation of risks

The data give concrete examples of how pride and identification with one's own idea, based on evaluation biases, may have another downside: It often leads to an underestimation of risks. The analysis shows that evaluation biases can equally lead to a loss of overview and focus, especially when it comes to individual inventors who are overwhelmed with one complete innovation task. This is said to be related to self-overestimation, which simply conceals problems. Another reason is again likely to be biases, such as the escalation of commitment (Staw, 1981) and the sunk cost effect (Arkes & Blumer, 1985), which at a certain point have no way back. Underestimation of risks is a good example of how a positive phenomenon can suddenly turn into a disadvantage (Table 4.3).

Table 4.3 Exemplifying quotes on "evaluation biases as a barrier"

EVALUATION BIASES AS A BARRIER	
Barriers to the quality of ideas	
Flawed understanding of the user	I sit in many self-created co-creation workshops (…) that just actually start with assumptions without ever validating or falsifying those assumptions. (I1)
Less effort for one's own things	When (…) I don't have that critical distance, I'm actually doing it for myself as I see fit. (A3)
	I got it, so it's good. But I don't try very hard to spread it, to upload it, to document it so that others can copy it. (A3)
Nonsense or mainstream ideas	The lack of critical distance—so that you end up having a mush, a group opinion, and then they (the co-creators) end up being tired and don't want to talk about it anymore. (A6)
	Experience gives us efficiency advantages, you see fixed patterns everywhere, at the same time it makes us less creative. (A1)
	If I don't critically reflect on this as a facilitator, as an enabler, I naturally have great potential to simply deliver nonsense. (I1)
Early fixation on unpromising concepts	I think the tendency is that because of the way we've been brought up and the way our school system has already worked, we're wired to jump into a solution very quickly. (I4)
	(…) Sometimes it was even noticeable that at the end of the workshop these people saw it as their contribution, that they had generated this one idea. And then it was more or less finished for them. (I3)
	Of course, everyone brings a backpack full of experience, knowledge about products, what they have seen. And best of all, they think they have the solution in their drawer, because it's practical. (I4)

(continued)

Table 4.3 (continued)

EVALUATION BIASES AS A BARRIER	
Barriers to the innovation process	
Loss of focus, time, and energy	(…) if you are already prototyping and then you realize that you have been talking about different things all the time, then you are getting into trouble (…) it will demotivate the whole team, it will delay the outcome, and everything. (I5)
	Biases cost time, process needs to go faster. (I6)
Destructive group dynamics	I think too much subjectivity usually leads to conflict within the group. Either you have a very mature group that can actually resolve conflict, because conflicts are good, right? (I5)
	If there are such dominant personalities in the workshop that they can really control and direct the whole mood and direction of the workshop. (A6)
	There are people who have a "need for nonconformism" (…) not because they are goal-oriented, but because they simply want to represent their own opinion (…) the subjectivity is very negative in this case. (A6)
Potential for frustration	Whether they overestimate themselves or not or whether they are in love with their own idea, not everybody is going to win. And the frustration that comes from that, they have to deal with that somehow (…) if you have a systematic bias to overestimate what you've created, that disappointment can be greater. (A1)
Underestimation of risks	People (…) who come to me with ideas, (…) what they do is often well thought out and good, you can also justify it, but many issues are typically always trivialized a bit, somehow seen in such an overly positive way (…) (A2)

4.4.3 Intersubjectivity

The dimension of intersubjectivity contains the concepts balancing methods, critical distance to own ideas, and empathy with the user. Multiple balancing methods and approaches for dealing with the negative impact of evaluation biases were identified and are summarized as *creativity methods, invitation to adopt a new perspective, involvement design, external assessment and catalyzation,* and *time pressure.* Critical distance to one's own ideas was found to *change with stages of the innovation process* and *to depend on given external factors.*

For the theme of empathy with the user, the data additionally revealed that this *empathy creates the basis for efficient innovation processes.* Between the positive and negative impacts of evaluation biases, the *critical turning point is defined as creating for oneself or for others.* The matter of whether the idea is intended for the co-creator themself (empowerment dimension "by me for one") or for others (empowerment dimension "by me for many") was clearly identified as a boundary. The concept of *intersubjectivity is learnable or unlearnable* demonstrates that intersubjectivity may be difficult or even impossible to learn. Intersubjectivity thus gains new relevance as a co-creation skill.

4.4.3.1 Balancing Methods

Creativity methods

A number of creativity techniques from practice can provide a critical distance to one's own creation and thus enable more intersubjectivity. The most mentioned concept was design thinking (Plattner et al., 2009). This six-step approach derived from the working processes of designers is a very suitable solution for creating critical distance and discarding biased ownership by focusing on the user, and for considering technological feasibility and economic viability. Beyond that, according to data, co-creators should ideally understand their mindset as a growth process and a continuous learning process. The data analysis points to other close links with design research, from which more concepts may be adopted in the future, such as critical distance to one's own work (Chong, 2013). The "kill your darlings" technique, a ritual letting-go of a favorite idea, is part of design thinking. This is seen as particularly helpful in creating critical distance. Another way to achieve this to use "thinking hats" (de Bono, 1990), where co-creators adopt predefined roles to gain new perspectives. A "future newspaper" may envision future outcomes and thinking innovation from the perspective of preferred results by writing a fictional report on the outcome of the idea. Simplifying an idea helps to clarify and change viewpoints through the "explain it to a layperson" method, in which the idea is presented to uninvolved individuals. A simple change of location to stimulate new ways of thinking is another example mentioned.

Invitation to adopt a new perspective

Besides the creativity methods described above, two more strategies for inviting co-creators to shift perspectives were derived: teamwork and early confrontation with users and market need. Both approaches use interaction to keep individual subjectivity at a minimum and reflection at a maximum from the outset. Working in groups can transform individual subjectivity into "group subjectivity," a kind of team spirit between co-creators, although not necessarily between co-creators and uninvolved other users (Cash et al., 2017; Ehkirch & Matsumae, 2024; Matsumae & Nagai, 2018). Early confrontation with users and market need can be achieved by early quantitative market tests. Design sprints (Knapp, 2016) are another suitable method for this purpose; they are an abbreviated five-day version of the design thinking process (Plattner et al., 2009). In addition, an interesting approach might be to create critical distance through constant interaction with other users on co-creation platforms. Intersubjectivity can be established easily by skillfully designing this interaction process.

Involvement design

Experts recommended creating critical distance by carefully designing the co-creator involvement, e.g., by giving clear specifications. In fact, the lack of intersubjectivity in its meaning of "shared understanding" (Cooper-White, 2014) is often a communication problem that can be solved by clearer guidelines. Indeed, most co-creators feel more comfortable in a more constrained environment, for example, through an exact formulation of the research question and the selection criteria for a good idea (Dahl & Moreau, 2007). There may still be questions about the transferability of all of the organizer's goals, benchmarks, and criteria, though this approach may significantly increase the likelihood of useful ideas.

When putting together a co-creation group, it is essential that all perspectives are included to provide balance. The most realistic co-creation results can be achieved with diversity in workshop groups, as equally recommended in theory by Schuurmann et al. (2015). Heterogeneity is the key to dealing with evaluation biases. The selection of co-creators is crucial to ensure that the composition of the team is socially and professionally appropriate to the task. This is more difficult than it seems at first glance: In addition to the different types of co-creators and their potential contributions, such as lead users, creative consumers, ordinary users, and emergent nature co-creators (Oßwald et al., 2019), organizers may additionally consider different possible biases, social skills, and the co-creators' ability for intersubjectivity, as shown with this study.

External assessment and catalyzation

One of the most frequently mentioned methods for dealing with evaluation biases was the external assessment and catalyzation of ideas, e.g., idea selection by the organizer of a crowdsourcing project or by experts in the relevant field (Haller et al., 2017). It is worth noting that external assessors may have the same biases as the original co-creators—even if it is simply the not-invented-here syndrome (Katz & Allen, 1982), which, even if not explicitly mentioned, may lie behind some expert statements. Equally, professional closeness can lead to a more critical attitude, the so-called novelty paradox (Boudreau et al., 2012). These aspects may be carefully observed when working with external assessors and possibly be considered when selecting them.

The selection of ideas can be biased, as described above. As an alternative, different individual ideas can be externally catalyzed into a consensual solution. Amabile's Consensual Assessment Technique (Amabile, 1982) is recommended for this purpose. This method uses individual assessments of experts in the respective domain, which are later collated to form a consensus. The technique is particularly suitable for identifying commonalities in individual tacit knowledge, one of the great strengths of open innovation (Terhorst et al., 2018), and combining them into an overall solution. The challenge in external assessment is to find suitable experts. According to data, this task can be carried out by intermediaries in their role as moderators. Likewise, professional designers can establish intersubjectivity through the incorporation of co-created ideas into their work. In this context, the approach of design-driven innovation (Verganti, 2009) is mentioned. Here, one individual designer takes on the role of catalyst, rather than several experts as is the case with the Consensual Assessment Technique. The concept of "design, when everybody designs" (Manzini, 2015) likewise follows this approach: Given that anyone can design today, the role of the designer has shifted to leading co-creation groups. Designers need to be very empathetic and bring strong visualization and processing skills to fulfill this new role.

Density and time pressure

Density and time pressure are found to be successful strategies for preventing evaluation biases caused by excessive reflection and discussion. Design sprints (Knapp, 2016) are particularly well suited for this purpose, according to intermediary experts. This five-phase, time-constrained derivation of the design thinking process (Plattner et al., 2009) offers the advantage of achieving results very quickly and in a structured way—and it generally enables intermediaries to manage evaluation biases where they are needed or where they are more of a barrier, e.g., preventing perfectionism or destructive group dynamics, or better involving more reluctant co-creators. Additionally, time pressure provides intermediaries with an argument to weed out unpromising ideas due to time constraints. In many innovating organizations, the task of assessing ideas is actually organized by intermediaries (Bessant & Rush, 1995).

4.4.3.2 Critical Distance to Own Ideas

Changes with stages of the innovation process

The expert interviews show that the need for co-creators to maintain a critical distance from their ideas increases if the idea is intended to be used by others. It appears that the need for distance changes with the stages of the innovation process. Evaluation biases are more needed in early innovation stages to foster creativity or to manage insecurities like fear of failure. Evaluation biases become barriers in later stages, such as prototyping, when more distance is required to allow review processes and confrontation with the user needs. In other words, at some point in the innovation process, it is necessary to move away from a purely subjective viewpoint if a market is to be developed beyond a single co-creator. This new contribution is not yet reflected in the theory.

Dependency on given external factors

According to the expert study, a number of given external factors influence the extent to which a balance of evaluation biases is necessary. These include different roles, such as that of the decision-maker in a co-creation team. Indeed, open innovation literature defines a whole range of actor roles, for example in living labs (Nyström et al., 2014). Linking these roles to their different needs for intersubjectivity may be an interesting new approach.

The expertise of the co-creators has an important influence: Professionalism, especially in the field of design, prevents undesirable evaluation biases. Thus, it can be derived that design amateurs may be less attractive for innovation co-creation than commonly assumed, such as in the concept of "amateur ideas of unobvious others" (Chesbrough, 2003; F. Piller et al., 2011). Conversely, a high level of expertise leads to a bias against novelty, such as in the novelty paradox (Boudreau et al., 2012), which describes how professional closeness to a scientific topic leads to a more critical attitude. Expert A5 emphasized that this phenomenon applies to every context, as in open innovation. A balanced solution between design amateurs and closed-minded experts would be to select expert co-creators from analogous markets for new product ideation (Franke et al., 2014).

A change of perspective in the form of critical distance seems much more difficult in a business-to-business (B2B) environment, due to the more complex, mostly technical interrelationships and the distance from the end user, as data show. Here, too, we are often dealing with a group of close professionals who are subject to biases such as the novelty paradox (Boudreau et al., 2012) and the not-invented-here syndrome (R. Katz & Allen, 1982). Thus, the impact of evaluation biases on open innovation may be considerably different in a business-only context. Overall, this varying need for critical distance at different stages of the innovation process, roles, expertise, and business environments may be related to the similarly varying commitment and valuation of consumer involvement (Atakan et al., 2014).

4.4.3.3 Empathy with the User

Empathy is the basis for an efficient innovation process

Open innovation does not work without empathy for the user. Empathy is the basis of an efficient innovation process. This empathy is not easy to achieve, as data analysis shows. Communication is essential to understanding needs and solutions. Individual reality is based on language, which always leaves room for interpretation. In addition, some needs may not be verbally communicable at all, and therefore may be a barrier to full empathy with users; this is known as sticky (von Hippel, 1994) and tacit knowledge (Cui & Wu, 2015). Therefore, like any innovation, it is almost impossible to objectively evaluate the results of innovation co-creation before they are on the market.

The critical turning point is creating for oneself or others

This interview study gives a remarkably consistent and striking answer to the question of when exactly the impact of evaluation biases turns from positive to negative: The matter of whether an idea is intended for the co-creator themself ("by me for one") or for others ("by me for others"). This defines a sharp boundary in the empowerment dimensions. Leaping beyond the individual into all three of the other fields where others are involved can make evaluation biases problematic. Co-creators design primarily for themselves. They do not necessarily consider whether their idea might be useful to others. This is particularly crucial in innovation co-creation, where the use of the idea by others is intended from the outset. In such cases, particular attention should be paid to the co-creators' ability to be intersubjective in order to avoid harmful biases.

Intersubjectivity is learnable or unlearnable

In contrast to the last concept, the interview study showed that there is no consensus on whether critical distance and thus intersubjectivity can be learned. The statements about whether it can be learned ranged from "with the right tools, you can teach it very quickly" (which again leads to the balancing methods), to "some can, some have a hard time" and "only a few can." The majority believed it is difficult to impossible. A learning process of self-evaluation in relation to others, e.g., through feedback, is similarly controversially discussed in the theory. According to the Dunning-Kruger effect (Kruger & Dunning, 1999), feedback does not induce learning, and intersubjectivity remains a static personal trait. This was later underpinned with another experiment (Schlösser et al., 2013). Other scientists (Galison,

1998; Krajc & Ortmann, 2008; Mayo et al., 2012) and practitioners (Murphy, 2017) strongly believe that learning effects exist regarding critical distance and intersubjectivity. It therefore remains an open question whether co-creators can actually be taught intersubjectivity, and how long it would take. With this in mind, it could make sense to look for this skill and select co-creators accordingly, in order to avoid laborious or even impossible learning processes (Table 4.4).

Table 4.4 Exemplifying quotes on "intersubjectivity"

INTERSUBJECTIVITY	
Balancing methods	
Creativity methods	Design thinking is the mindset—the basic principles of how to empathetically generate innovation. By focusing on the desirability of the user, but of course also considering the technological feasibility and economic viability in the process. (I1)
	(…) there is a process there called kill-your-darlings. (…)That's the first thing I have to think about right now, to create a distance to this self-image. I think that it is exactly this problem that needs to be discarded, this ownership. (I3)
	Everyone is in the daily business. What we do (are) (…) topics where we take customers to other places. So really not office, but (…) Hotel, mountain lodge or whatever. (I4)
Invitation to adopt a new perspective	That I get the critical distance much faster through constant interaction with the other users on the platform. (A4)
	I think one way we solved this was to work a lot in groups (…)Then this leads to the fact that in this group a certain distance is also established, because of course the discussion starts in the group and this feeling of love does not break out in one head (…) if I work on it alone. (I3)
	One thing we do early on with teams is to get quantitative results, so that means we early on will try to actually test it in the market—build MVPs, do online advertisements, build landing pages, proof of concept, these kind of things, and that will always show at some point, whether those biases that you might have had in the beginning, are true or not. (I2)

(continued)

Table 4.4 (continued)

INTERSUBJECTIVITY	
Involvement design	(…) yes, there is a lack (of intersubjectivity), because it actually always requires concrete exercises of concrete work instructions to break exactly this subjectivity. (I1)
	(…) if, for example, the task is, please build me the logo that best suits me, best reflects our goal or most captivates the customers or the target group and takes them along. That's different than if you were to say artistically: and now build a logo that you like best. (A5)
	That's a core challenge, to put together a good co-creation team, and then I have to make sure that the individual blinders still form a good picture together. (I1)
	I think it plays a role there, how diverse the group is and how strong the individuals are. (I4)
External assessment and catalyzation	At some point, a certain decision maker has to make an announcement (…) and that is also a subjective opinion. (I1)
	So if I collect concrete ideas (…) and each of the designers says to themself, "Wow, that's the most beautiful and best logo there has ever been," then it doesn't matter to me as the organizer at first, because as long as they submit it and as long as I can choose, I can say, "But I'm not going to take (…) a logo from you, I'm going to take another one." (A1)
	Either I have a voting mechanism that's a crowd vote, if the crowd thinks it's great, fine, and if they don't, I can turn them off immediately, because I don't really care as a host if they don't meet my requirements, I don't see the problem with that. (A4)
Density and time pressure	But it is not discussed for long. Just to speed things up and prevent certain effects, such as someone owning this co-creation workshop for themselves and then no one asking anyone else what they want, (…) (I1)
	I think that's an advantage because you're not thinking long and hard about how to make something look perfect. (I2)
	I'm more of a fan of saying: We'll give you five minutes, write down all the ideas, even if they're crazy, and do challenges and evaluate them all. (I4)

(continued)

Table 4.4 (continued)

INTERSUBJECTIVITY	
Critical distance to own ideas	
Change with stages of innovation process	And then in different stages. For instance, especially in the beginning, I guess, deep emotional involvement for everybody is more important to overcome this fear of failure, basically. (…) So you need a stronger emotional bond, while later it might be actually useful to let go of your cognitive binding to a degree that you can actually review what you have already done. That you can step out of the creator's mindset, and step into the reviewer's mindset, which is very different. (I5)
Dependency on given external factors	(…) but he must then subjectively decide "Bam, run." That is then the role of the decision-maker. Maybe you also have to define a few roles like that. Who should be subjective and how? (I1)
	I saw this effect (…) almost exclusively with my customers who don't have a design background. (I3)
	These different considerations apply to any context, including science. (…) topics that I am more familiar with, I may be more critical towards news like non-novelty bias. (A5)
	And I think the change of perspective, that is (…) too often too seldom made (…) B2B environment in particular. I think B2C is easier. (I4)
	Also, co-creation in B2B is more difficult, as it's more difficult to create a creative discussion about a very technical subject (I6)
Empathy with the user	
Empathy is the basis for an efficient innovation process	If you have a lack of empathy for your potential user, I think that has the potential to have negative effects more than anything else. (I1)
	But I think what always lacks, if it's pure design thinking and pure co-creation, it's the validation of the market. And that will also be the proof in the end. (I2)
	How I see, the issue is that basically we create our reality based on language, mostly. Our intersubjective reality. And this is pretty much the whole problem, or where the problem comes into life. Because words and sentences always leave room for interpretation. In design processes, in creative processes, co-creation processes, you have to find a way, to get a, (…) depending on which stage, maybe, minimal or maximum overlap in the intersubjectivity that we experience. (I5)

(continued)

Table 4.4 (continued)

INTERSUBJECTIVITY	
The critical turning point is creating for oneself or others	If I customize my t we used -shirt online (…) then I can totally fall in love with it, whether others find it awesome is all the same. But then (…) in the end it's all about myself. (I1)
	Actually, it becomes at most critical, if one depends on the valuation of other persons and this differs from the own (…) In other words, if it is used instrumentally, the product, and not for oneself. (A1)
Intersubjectivity is learnable or unlearnable	And you notice quite quickly that after five or six workshops or a design sprint (…) That a very good distance can be created there, and that's something you can teach people well. (I3)
	(…) I can distance myself from what I have done or I can take the perspective of others, that is certainly a characteristic of a person, some are better at it, some are worse at it. You can certainly learn it, it's both. (A3)
	(…) to answer your question (after a learning process): you can, but it takes time and depends on the type of person. (I4)
	I think few can do that. (A5)

4.5 Discussion

Balancing subjective views on intersubjectivity can be seen as a basis for efficient innovation processes. This interview study contributes to a comprehensive explanation of intersubjectivity and critical distance from one's own creation, as well as to practical balancing strategies in open innovation. Evaluation biases impact the practice of open innovation in many ways: as a need, as a barrier, and with intersubjectivity as a balance between the two. This study sheds light on all aspects of evaluation biases and contributes to a comprehensive theoretical explanation of this topic.

4.5.1 From a Research Perspective

Moving away from an individual perspective of evaluation to intersubjectivity as a shared and realistic understanding of the evaluation, e.g., of an idea, may be adapted to open innovation from social sciences and design research (Amabile, 1983; Cash et al., 2017; Cooper-White, 2014; Ehkirch & Matsumae, 2024; Matsumae & Nagai, 2018; Shapin, 2017).

Experts pointed to other close links with design research, from which more concepts may be adopted in the future, such as critical distance to one's own work (Chong, 2013). The term "intersubjectivity" was not known to all experts before the introductory discussion in the interviews. Nonetheless, the data analysis revealed a variety of balancing strategies from practice to achieve it. Some of these have not yet made their way into open innovation literature. It could be beneficial to integrate these.

Need for critical distance changes with roles and stages of the innovation process

There is a varying need for critical distance in open innovation. In some cases, it can be beneficial; in others, it can be detrimental. With regard to different roles, it is particularly important that decision-makers have a certain critical distance in order to perform appropriately. The need for critical distance varies with the stages of the innovation process. While evaluation biases are more helpful in early stages, a greater critical distance is needed for a more realistic assessment in later phases closer to the market. These results are not yet reflected in the theory and may add interesting aspects to concepts such as the similarly stage-dependent consumer involvement (Atakan et al., 2014).

Creating for oneself or for others is the turning point between positive and negative impacts of evaluation biases

It was found that evaluation biases can make the co-creators perform even better. The same evaluation biases, however, can lead them to close themselves off and put less effort into their own creation. This new and rather contradictory insight may lie at the critical turning point between positive and negative impacts of evaluation biases: creating for oneself ("by me for one") or creating for others ("by me for others"). This finding extends recent knowledge on intersubjectivity frameworks (Maier & Baccarella, 2024), such as the co-creator empowerment dimensions, and is particularly relevant to co-creation for innovation theory, where the use of the idea by others is inherent.

Intersubjectivity could be unlearnable

The results suggest that intersubjectivity could be hard to learn or not learnable at all. This may give a new spin to the previous inconclusive literature on its learnability (Galison, 1998; Krajc & Ortmann, 2008; Kruger & Dunning, 1999; Schlösser et al., 2013). Moreover, theory may want to add the ability for intersubjectivity to the set of selection criteria for co-creators, as it is probably a static trait for efficiency in open innovation. This could be integrated into co-creation concepts such as the lead user (von Hippel, 1986) or the emergent nature co-creator (Hoffman et al., 2010).

4.5.2 From a Managerial Perspective

A holistic understanding of the role of evaluation biases may be essential for practitioners. With more knowledge about such biases, they can avoid pitfalls and adapt their processes to get the best ideas out of open innovation. Organizers can understand evaluation biases as a two-sided issue. Theory has already shown many benefits of evaluation biases, such as customers' emotional bonding, resulting in better identification with co-created products and thus higher purchase intentions, more willingness to pay, and better customer satisfaction and recommendations (Schreier et al., 2013). The following therefore focusses on the new aspects found in this study.

Evaluation biases give co-creators resilience
To gain more flexibility in co-creation processes, managers may foster feelings of ownership and commitment in the co-creators to motivate, build a relationship with the organizer, and maintain the perceived individual ownership of an idea across groups and time periods. This induces perseverance in overcoming risks or other challenges during the further innovation process.

Evaluation biases affect all individual roles
Practitioners may keep in mind that, despite all the benefits, stimulating evaluation biases in co-creators can be risky. It might create higher potential for frustration and dissatisfaction, and result in undesirable reactions like idle and closed-off behavior. Evaluation biases can affect all roles: co-creators, intermediaries, experts, and even individuals in the innovating organization. This may negatively affect the risk assessment and particularly the selection of co-created ideas by the organizer or experts.

Select and involve co-creators on the basis of intersubjectivity
Selection criteria for co-creators could include their ability for intersubjectivity, as it may be difficult or even impossible to learn. If the creation is intended for people other than individual co-creators, their intersubjectivity skills become even more crucial. The need for intersubjectivity is greater in later innovation stages

and decision-making roles. Constant interaction with other users and working in diverse teams can additionally promote intersubjectivity. Skillful involvement design can help manage the intersubjectivity of co-creators by selecting and moderating participants according to their personalities, providing clear specifications, and encouraging focus on the innovation goal with density and time pressure. In addition, balancing methods and approaches to deal with the negative impact of evaluation biases were identified, such as creativity methods (e.g., design thinking, "kill your darlings," change of location), an invitation to adopt a new perspective through teamwork and early confrontation with users and market need, involvement design (e.g., clear specifications, selection and diversity of co-creators), catalyzation of ideas and external assessment (e.g., Consensual Assessment Technique), and density and time pressure (e.g., design sprints). These methods and tools provide practitioners with a comprehensive overview of how to proactively deal with evaluation biases, especially when pursuing innovation co-creation for new ideas rather than tapping into sticky user knowledge.

4.5.3 Summary of Findings

This expert interview study shows that the need for critical distance changes with the roles in innovation co-creation and the stages of the innovation process. It is particularly important that decision-makers maintain a critical distance to the innovation project in order to perform appropriately. Critical distance is additionally needed in later stages of the innovation process, closer to the market. In contrast, evaluation biases were found to be helpful in early phases. In addition to having varying impact at different stages of the innovation process, evaluation biases impact differently across the empowerment dimensions of co-creators. Creating for oneself or for others is defined as the turning point between positive and negative impacts of evaluation biases. The data analysis furthermore uncovered new aspects of evaluation biases that have received little consideration to date. Evaluation biases positively influence innovation processes by giving co-creators resilience in overcoming risks and other challenges. The negative influence of evaluation biases goes further than has been recognized to date. It is important to keep in mind that evaluation biases can affect all individual roles, not only co-creators, as a barrier to the success of innovation co-creation projects. Moreover, since the data analysis showed that intersubjectivity might be unlearnable, motivating different roles to be more intersubjective for a better transfer of individual solution ideas may be challenging. Exploring the learnability of intersubjectivity in more depth may therefore be a promising avenue for further research.

YOUR ITEMS FROM STUDY II

- The need for critical distance changes with roles and stages of the innovation process.
- Creating for oneself or for others is the turning point between positive and negative impacts of evaluation biases.
- Evaluation biases give co-creators resilience.
- Evaluation biases can affect all individual roles as a barrier.
- Intersubjectivity might be unlearnable.

5 Study III: Experimenting with Intersubjectivity in the Laboratory

Supplementary Information The online version contains supplementary material available at https://doi.org/10.1007/978-3-658-48890-1_5.

M. Oßwald, *When Co-Creation Leads to Love*, Markt- und Unternehmensentwicklung Markets and Organisations,
https://doi.org/10.1007/978-3-658-48890-1_5

Intersubjectivity might be essential for open innovation efficiency, especially if the creation is intended for people other than individual co-creators. The interviewed experts from the previous chapter are divided on whether intersubjectivity is learnable in an open innovation context. Study III[1] now explores the learning of intersubjectivity in greater depth in a laboratory experiment. The present work uses a wide range of intersubjectivity measurements, creativity tests, and various analysis methods to investigate possible learning effects.

5.1 Research Objective

To efficiently activate the significant potential of creative amateurs in open innovation, it is important to know the boundaries and mechanisms of this potential. When it comes to selecting suitable co-creators for innovation processes with increased quality, it is still unclear whether intersubjectivity is a measurable personal trait that should be used as a selection criterion for co-creators in open innovation processes, or if it is a learnable skill. The likelihood of obtaining intersubjective co-creators would increase if intersubjectivity could be learned. In the course of identifying evaluation biases from the literature review in Chap. 1, some suggestions about respective traits or learning mechanisms were found, and will be investigated further in this study.

In open innovation, learning processes for skills are usually triggered by feedback (Roth et al., 2017). If intersubjectivity was a skill, it would be learnable in an open innovation context. The Dunning-Kruger effect (Kruger & Dunning, 1999), however, assumes that feedback does not induce learning, and that intersubjectivity remains a static personal trait. The test underlying this effect identifies overestimators, correct estimators, and underestimators in four static performance groups, which are defined by external assessment. The allocation to performance groups is not considered dynamic. This was later underpinned with another experiment (Schlösser et al., 2013).

Experiments on the overconfidence effect (Pallier et al., 2002) identified confidence as a trait that relies, to a small extent, on an individual's cognitive ability. A subsequent study on the topic found that overestimating oneself is context-dependent and people tend to overestimate their ability to do simple tasks, such

[1] Study III is based on the 2020 experimental seminar and unpublished seminar paper "Creativity at Work" conducted at the Laboratory for Experimental Research LERN in Nuremberg (Germany).

as driving (Moore & Healy, 2008). Here, overconfidence is defined in three different ways: (a) overestimation of one's actual performance, (b) overestimation of one's performance relative to others, and (c) excessive precision in one's beliefs (Moore & Healy, 2008, p. 502). The context in case a) can likewise be understood as self-centered, such as "by me for one," while the relationship to others in b) can be understood in a setting such as "by me for many" in the empowerment dimensions (Maier & Baccarella, 2024).

On the other hand, other researchers and practitioners assume that the repetition of tasks, combined with financial incentives and feedback, can certainly produce learning effects in self-assessment, albeit with a certain amount of effort (Krajc & Ortmann, 2008; Murphy, 2017). According to another long-term study by Mayo et al. (2012), in addition to the factor of repetition, there is the factor of time, which is needed to translate feedback into self-awareness and ultimately learning. Such learning can take different amounts of time, depending on gender (Mayo et al., 2012). This insight from learning theory notes that unexpected feedback may be accompanied by an unpleasant experience. Depending on the level of discomfort, self-awareness might not even occur at all (Mezirow, 1991). It is still unclear whether intersubjectivity can be learned through feedback in an open innovation context. Study III therefore explores the following research question:

RQ III: Can co-creators learn intersubjectivity through feedback?

5.2 Research Design: Laboratory Experiment

A quantitative approach using laboratory experimental methodology with a pretest–posttest control group design with randomization was selected as suitable to answer the research question in this study. This method offers high internal validity (MacCoun, 2003) for discriminating between alternative theories, such as the indecisive theories of learning intersubjectivity. It additionally provides an accurate and statistically unbiased view of the effect of an intervention, such as feedback (MacCoun, 2003). The goal of the experiment was to examine the assessment of co-creation tasks by other participants and by the participants themselves, and then to determine intersubjectivity using the differences in the assessments. Thereby, possible learning effects were investigated using a variety of intersubjectivity measures, creativity tests, and different analysis methods.

5.2.1 Measurements of Intersubjectivity

A prerequisite for determining the learnability of intersubjectivity is its measurement. For long-term co-designing groups, Ehkirch and Matsumae (2024) suggest that the intersubjective level P of co-creators is measured over a time period of a dynamic context that lies between two static states with the equation $P(n + 1) = P(n) + \Delta P$. The static data come from interpersonal factors like subjective feedback, behavior observations, and measurements of bio signals. Interpersonal factors deliver the dynamic data. This model mainly considers the processes among grouped co-creators over a longer time, so it is not fully suited to measuring intersubjectivity beyond the co-creator group—for example, in the empowerment dimension "by me for many" (Maier & Baccarella, 2024). It does not clearly identify intersubjectively skilled co-creators or their individual learning processes, as it considers intersubjectivity more as a phenomenon of group dynamics.

The dual-measures equation with intermediate subjective feedback may provide a basis for further investigation of measuring intersubjectivity between co-creators and users. Intersubjectivity might be measured by the extent to which others assign the same score to the ideas and, if they are informed, to what extent the co-creators move in the direction of the assessment by others in a second self-assessment. Thus, in the laboratory experiment, feedback about the assessments of others served as a treatment variation given to participants before they assessed their own designs. Moreover, the laboratory experiment takes advantage of a specific feature of innovation co-creation: that co-creators can combine the roles of creator and potential user in one person. Co-creators must consciously switch between these two roles in order to establish intersubjectivity with (other) users, which is the focus of this thesis. The second role of the participants as potential users of the creations makes it possible to use mutual assessments as feedback. This may enable the investigation of how feedback can influence intersubjectivity between co-creators and users through mutual assessment. Since this is a new approach, further self-assessment scales regarding self-criticism and creativity assessment were explored for control through a pre- and posttest. A review of self-report measures (Rose & Rimes, 2018) shows that most self-assessment scales based on self-criticism measure dysfunctional forms of negative self-evaluation, often related to clinical psychology (e.g., predisposition to depression). Other measures are quite time-consuming, e.g. the temperament and personality scale with 109 items incorporating ten subscales, with just one being self-assessment (Parker et al., 2006). Some measures focus more on negative self-processing rather than work/achievement processing

(Ishiyama & Munson, 1993). For the purposes of this study, the investigated self-assessment scales associated with criticism seemed not to be appropriate. Most of them measure psychological traits associated with dysfunction rather than an individual's ability to reflect in the sense of intersubjectivity.

Instead of self-criticism, intersubjectivity could be seen in connection with the creativity of co-creators, as this concept originates from creativity research (Chong, 2013). It makes sense to attribute intersubjectivity to creative consumers (Berthon et al., 2011) or, more generally, to attribute intersubjectivity to creativity as a selection criterion for co-creators (Bogers et al., 2017). As co-creation is closely related to design and is therefore based on creativity, methods for assessing creativity were further investigated for their possible use in this study. This type of assessment is often done with self-report scales (Silvia et al., 2012). Table 5.1 gives an overview of reviewed creativity tests.

Table 5.1 Overview of reviewed creativity tests

LEVEL	AUTHOR and YEAR	CREATIVITY MEASUREMENT
(1) Trait / self-rated	**Hocevar 1980** Carson et al. (2005) Goff & Torrance (2002) Cropley & Cropley (2005) Batey (2007)	**Creative Behavior Inventory (CBI)** Creative Achievement Questionnaire (CAQ) Abbreviated Torrance Test Four-dimensional model Biographical Inventory of Creative Behaviors (BICB)
(2) Trait / objective	Williams (1980)	Williams Creativity Test (Part C)
(3) Product / other-rated	Amabile (1982) Kaufman et al. (2007) **O'Quin & Besemer (2006)** **Williams (1980)**	Consensual Assessment Technique (CAT) **Creative Product Semantic Scale (CPSS)** **Williams Creativity Test (Part A)**
(4) Process / self-rated and objective	Bissola & Imperator (2011)	Qualitative Content Analysis

Recent literature generally identifies nine different creativity measures. These are grouped according to the level at which creativity is measured. The levels are defined as a personality trait, either by self-report (1), in which individuals answer a series of questions, or by objective measurement (2), in which a group of trained researchers rate tasks completed by an individual expert according to predefined criteria (Batey, 2012), e.g., in the Williams Creativity Test (Williams, 1980).

Another way to measure creativity is by assessing the characteristics of the creation (3). Creativity can be viewed from a process/organizational perspective (4). The focus here is on the effectiveness of the integrative approach in which *"individual creative skills, team dynamics, and organizational solutions interact to produce a collective creative performance"* (Bissola et al., 2014, p. 77).

For this study, pre- and posttest procedures were selected from the list above that could be administered quickly and easily without further external expertise. To fit the laboratory environment, an abbreviated Williams Creativity Test Part A (Williams, 1980) was chosen as an other-rated pretest and an introduction to the tasks of designing icons. Selected questions from the Creative Behavior Inventory (Hocevar, 1980) were chosen as a self-rated posttest, being a popular measure of creativity. A modified version of the Creative Product Semantic Scale (O'Quin & Besemer, 1989) served as a basis for the assessment to test a broad range of rating dimensions for their suitability for measuring intersubjectivity.

5.2.2 Experimental Procedure

The laboratory experiment was designed to find out if co-creators can learn intersubjectivity through feedback on two co-creative tasks. It was conducted with two groups, each comprised of 20 randomly assigned participants. The feedback group received feedback from other participants on their co-creative task, while the control group did not. This was in order to find possible treatment effects of the feedback. The experimental procedure took place in an experimental laboratory using computers. After assessing Task 1, all participants in the no-feedback control group immediately began working on Task 2. The feedback group received treatment in an additional step between the assessment of Task 1 and Task 2, as shown in Fig. 5.1. The co-creative tasks were to design two icons with a specific black-and-white drawing application. Task 1 was to design an application icon for "screenshot," and Task 2 was to design an application icon for "mobile payment." To enhance the results for a possible connection between creativity and intersubjectivity, the creativity of the participants was investigated in a pretest and a posttest. All stages are described in detail in the following sections.

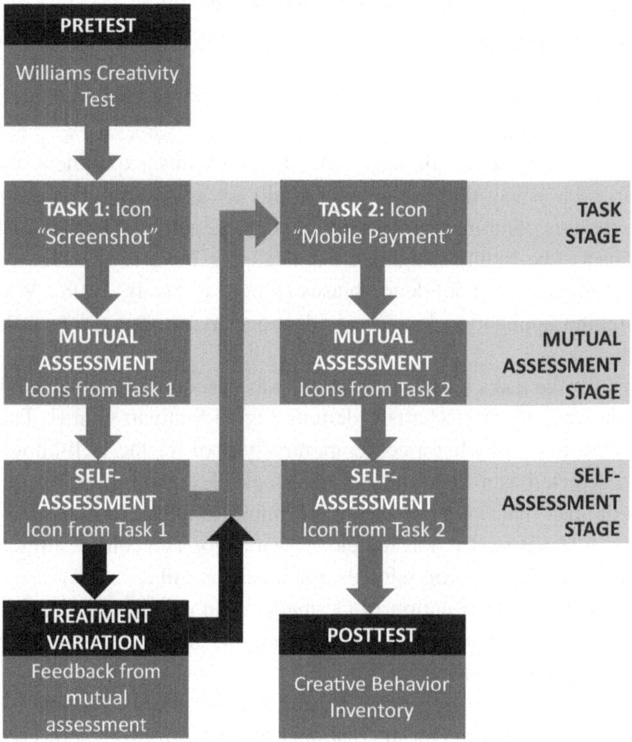

Fig. 5.1 Structure of the laboratory experiment. (Author's illustration)

5.2.2.1 Pretest

The William's Creativity Test (Williams, 1980) was conducted as a pretest before the experiment, as a paper and pencil test. The idea of this test was to assess and control for the individual creativity level. Participants were asked to creatively complete abstract forms—by drawing—that were presented inside boxes. In addition, they were asked to give a title to each of the sketches. This served as an introduction to the later design of icons in the tasks. Considering the time limitation of the whole experiment, the original full version of the test was shortened to eight sketches, instead of 12, in just eight minutes. This part of the experiment was not incentivized and did not influence other parts. The evaluation of the test was conducted by using the original William's Creativity Test scale (Williams, 1980) after both groups had completed the experiment. The evaluation criteria were fluency, flexibility, originality, elaboration, and titles. A list of chosen criteria and an explanation can be found in Appendix C and Appendix D in the Electronic Supplementary Material.

5.2.2.2 Task Stage

Given the mutual assessment stage, the tasks in this experiment had to be designed in such a way that participants could act as experts in assessing them, just as co-creators combine the roles of creator and potential user in one person. The tasks had to be intuitive and self-explanatory (Greve et al., 2016), and easy to learn to mitigate overconfidence biases (Moore & Healy, 2008). With this in mind, designing application icons was identified as an appropriate task for this experiment.

The idea for the tasks in this experiment was based on the "Speichern unter… ?" competition run by Wirtschaftsförderung Region Stuttgart GmbH. The competition aimed to find out what a contemporary symbol for the well-known "Save" icon, often depicted as a floppy disk, might look like. The reason for the competition was the fact that floppy disks are becoming obsolete, having been replaced by hard drives, USB sticks, and the cloud years ago. The contest attracted 1,847 submissions from design professionals and amateurs alike.

It gained nationwide attention in Germany as an example of usability design where amateurs, as users of icons, contributed quite similar work of equal quality to professional submissions[2].

Since Otl Aicher's pictographic design for the 1972 Olympic Games in Munich, icons have become an internationally standardized form of communication beyond language[3]. The introduction of graphical user interfaces on computers and other electronic devices (such as smartphones) made icons an integral part of people's everyday lives, be it in the design of computer program icons or emoticons such as the smiley face (Abdullah & Hübner, 2005). On the one hand, icons can be used to transfer information independent of language and as quickly as

[2] Initially planned as a local competition, "Speichern unter… ?" gained national attention in the design community when it featured in advertising and design magazines like W&V: https://www.wuv.de/Archiv/Designwettbewerb-So-könnte-das-neue-%22Speichern%22-Icon-aussehen.

The winning icons can be seen here: https://www.stuttgarter-zeitung.de/gallery.wettbewerb-speichern-unter-die-favoriten-fuer-ein-neues-icon-stehen-fest.35b61a8a-0936-4558-a7df-29b42b141fa0.html.

[3] Otl Aicher's design for the 1972 Olympic Games in Munich is considered a breakthrough for the worldwide use of icons. He is called "the father of the geometric man". See www.piktogramm.de.

possible, thus serving as a low-barrier means of communication. On the other hand, their use is an easy way to convey information, such as ideas, regardless of design skills (Urban, 1995). The simple form of communication through icons is ideal for communication between the two roles of creator and user.

The tasks in the present laboratory experiment were therefore to create two sequential icon designs with a specific drawing application on the computers in the laboratory. The icon had to be drawn in black and white on a canvas grid of 30*30 pixels. Black-and-white drawing on a grid system typically results in an easily understandable and comparable representation of the tasks (Urban, 1995), regardless of drawing skills. A screenshot of the icon drawing application can be found in Appendix E in the Electronic Supplementary Material.

The experiment procedure followed two main objectives when choosing the icons for the task stage:

- The design of the icon has not been used before, so there is not already a known design for the icon.
- All participants should be familiar with the concept of the icon, so they understand what they are being asked to create.

Based on these main objectives, two application icon designs were chosen for the task stage: an icon for the "screenshot" function for Task 1 and an icon for the "mobile payment" function for Task 2. The duration of a task was defined after conducting a pilot session, which determined the time needed to complete the drawing. Explanations of the two tasks are presented below.

- **Task 1:** *"Create a new icon for the screenshot function. Think of it as an icon that could be used for capturing an image of the display of an electronic device such as a smartphone. Try to create a new design that has not been used before."*
- **Task 2:** *"Create a new icon for the mobile payment function. Think of it as an icon that allows users to pay for a product or service on a portable electronic device. Try to create a new design that has not been used before."*

5.2.2.3 Mutual Assessment Stage

During the mutual assessment stage, the participants were asked to rate five randomly selected icon designs from other participants, for both icon creation tasks. The assessment of the icon designs is based on the Creative Product Semantic Scale for assessing the creativity of products as introduced by O'Quin and Besemer (1989). This test was primarily chosen to find a suitable measurement dimension for intersubjectivity. The scale was modified in two aspects to fit the procedure. First, in order to make the experiment less time-consuming, the number of assessment dimensions was reduced. Based on reliability measures and factor analyses from the corresponding publication, two subscales in each of the three dimensions (novelty, resolution, elaboration, and synthesis) were selected for their particularly strong correlation with the overall score for the corresponding dimension and their possible contribution of reliable measures across participants. Within each subscale, the most appropriate criteria for the task stage were selected. Overall, six assessment dimensions were chosen for the mutual assessment stage: *fresh, surprising, logical, functional, understandable,* and *well-crafted.* The chosen criteria and an explanation of each are shown in Table 5.2. Next, the original 0–7 scale was expanded to a 0–10 Likert scale to ensure comparability with other related experiments.

Table 5.2 Selected assessment dimensions after O'Quin and Besemer (1989)

ASSESSMENT DIMENSIONS	
FRESH	Would you consider the design a "fresh" design or is it rather overused?
SURPRISING	Does the design contain surprising elements or was the icon design predictable?
LOGICAL	Do you see a logical relationship between the icon and the activity or device it is supposed to symbolize?
FUNCTIONAL	Is the design of the icon functional, i.e. does it focus on providing an easily comprehensible symbol, or is it non-functional, i.e. does it contain elements which do not serve this function.
UNDERSTANDABLE	Is it easy to understand what the icon is supposed to symbolize or does it need further explanation?
WELL-CRAFTED	Is the icon design well-crafted or rather crude or rudimentary?

5.2.2.4 Self-assessment Stage

In order to calculate intersubjectivity, participants were asked to assess their own icon designs. Because people tend to act under an assumed desired behavior (Fisher, 1993; Luchs et al., 2010), no direct self-evaluation was used for the estimation. Participants tend to assess themselves more favorably than others, and weigh their own intentions more heavily (Alicke & Govorun, 2005; Kruger & Gilovich, 2004). Here, participants were asked to reveal their estimates of the average assessment that other participants would assign to the icon designs, using the "projective technique" of asking participants to identify which product the "average person" would prefer (Fisher, 1993). Participants were asked to estimate the average assessments assigned to their icons by the other participants, using the same 0–10 scale as in the mutual assessment stage for each of the six criteria. After receiving the estimates, their intersubjective level (P) was calculated as the distance between the average mutual assessments (AMA) that icon designs received from the other participants, and the self-assessment (SA) estimates in the absolute value with the following equation based on Ehkirch and Matsumae (2024) at a fixed measuring point in time t: $P_t = SA_t - AMA_t$

The self-assessment SA is defined as a "sufficiently precise estimate" if it is located in the given interval [AMA − 1, AMA + 1], which means it is within the radius of one point from the true average assessment. An example of the "sufficiently precise" estimate is presented in Fig. 5.2, where the self-assessment SA = 4.5 points is within the radius of [AMA − 1, AMA + 1] from the average mutual assessment AMA = 5.2 points.

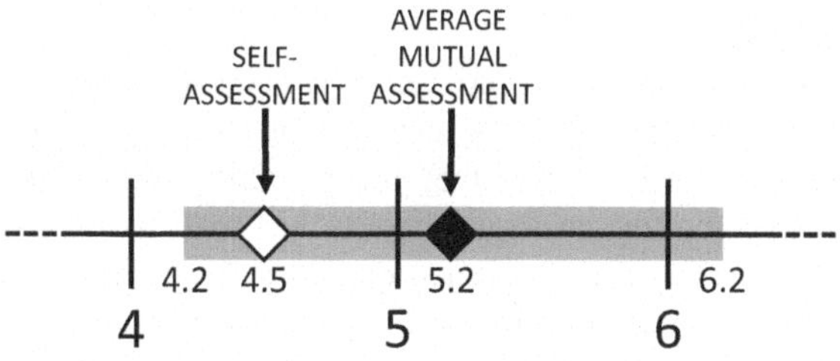

Fig. 5.2 Example of a "sufficiently precise" estimate

In order to truthfully elicit participants' beliefs about the average mutual assessment, the experimental procedure relied on the simple belief elicitation mechanism (Schlag & Tremewan, 2016). Thus, the "sufficiently precise" estimates were incentivized with a "precision bonus."

5.2.2.5 Treatment Variation

The treatment was designed to determine whether intersubjectivity can be learned through feedback. This would mean that feedback affects an individual's self-assessment in terms of more precise estimations in the future and/or by self-assessment moving towards the feedback.

It is therefore suspected that participants will assess their own designs more precisely after receiving feedback on their creations, which leads to the first hypothesis:

Hypothesis 1: *"Receiving feedback on one's creation is associated with more precise self-assessment in the future."*

By separating the participants who tend to overestimate and underestimate the quality of their own creation before and after receiving feedback, a test can show whether they change their self-assessment behavior.

It is hypothesized that after receiving the feedback, overestimators will decrease their self-assessment, and underestimators will increase their self-assessments of their second icon designs.

Hypothesis 2: *"Participants react to feedback by changing their behavior by adapting their self-assessment to the average mutual assessment."*

5.2.2.6 Posttest

After the second self-assessment stage, each participant was asked to fill out a final questionnaire as a posttest. The first part of the questionnaire was about control questions to check whether they had any difficulties during the experiment. The second part of the questionnaire was the Creativity Behavior Inventory (Hocevar, 1980). It consisted of selected questions designed to obtain an additional measure of the creativity level of the participants, as shown in Appendix F in the Electronic Supplementary Material. The last part was designed to assess the general characteristics of participants and included questions about their sociodemographics.

5.2.2.7 Incentivization

To achieve its full creative potential, innovation co-creation is typically based on the intrinsic motivation of the co-creators (Kristensson et al., 2008; Mochon et al., 2012). As it was difficult for participants in this experiment to relate closely to the project due to randomization and the laboratory environment, they were incentivized for their motivation and full participation. All participants were awarded €4.00 for showing up on time. They could earn an additional €8.00 for a higher average mutual assessment than a randomly selected other participant, who was not involved in the mutual assessment of the other. This was done to motivate the participants to make more creative contributions to the task. The self-assessment stage was moreover incentivized to encourage participants to provide more precise self-assessments, i.e., intersubjectivity. If their estimation in one of the six Creative Product Semantic Scale assessment dimensions was "sufficiently precise," the participants received a precision bonus of €2.50. Since two assessment dimensions were randomly selected for incentive purposes, the maximum possible precision bonus for one participant was €5.00.

5.2.3 Experimental Protocol

The experiment took place at the Laboratory for Experimental Research (LERN) in Nuremberg and was conducted with the software tool z-Tree (Fischbacher, 2007). The recruiting tool ORSEE (Greiner, 2015) was used to organize student participants. In total, 40 participants took part in the experiment. The target group were bachelor's and master's students from Friedrich-Alexander-Universität Erlangen-Nürnberg (FAU). They were divided into two groups of 20 participants and randomly assigned to partitioned computers. The experimental procedure was conducted identically in all sessions.

At the beginning of each stage of the experiment, the instructions were given to participants to familiarize them with the requirements of each stage. All participants made their decisions in full anonymity. Before the start of Creative Task 1, participants had two minutes to learn how the drawing tool worked. In addition, to ensure that all participants understood the rules of the experiment, the sheets with control questions were provided to them before the start of every stage. All questions during the workshop were answered by the conducting researcher personally. The experiment with each of the two groups took approximately 1.5 hours.

5.2.4 Data Collection and Analysis

All data from this study were collected in the software z-Tree, where the statistical analysis took place. The analyzed variables are defined in Table 5.3. The wording "Icon 1" is used for Task 1, and "Icon 2" is used for Task 2.

Table 5.3 Definition of variables

VARIABLE	ABBREVIATION	DESCRIPTION	RANGE
Average mutual assessment	AMA	The average of scores given by other participants to the respective icon (2 icons) in the respective dimension (6 dimensions).	0–10
Average mutual assessment (total)	AMAT	The average of the sum of scores for all dimensions given by other participants to the respective icon (2 icons).	0–60
Self-assessment	SA	Subjects' own score for the respective icon (2 icons) in the respective dimension (6 dimensions).	0–10
Self-assessment (total)	SAT	The sum of own scores.	0–60

The data collection included the following sources:

- **Data directly collected in z-Tree:** All self-assessment and mutual assessment data were directly collected and processed in the software. Data from the posttest were additionally directly collected in z-Tree.
- **Data from a paper and pencil test:** The data of the pretest were imported into the software after a manual evaluation by the researcher. The evaluation was conducted under the criteria *fluency, flexibility, originality, elaboration,* and *titles* from the original Williams Creativity Test scale (Williams, 1980). A closer explanation of the criteria and an example of the test can be seen in Appendix C and Appendix D in the Electronic Supplementary Material.

The data analysis began with the compilation of the data and the calculation of mean values and possible correlations. This was done in the same way for both the feedback group and the control group. First, the scores of the self-assessment were analyzed in all six assessment dimensions: *fresh, surprising, logical, functional, understandable,* and *well-crafted.* Then, in order to determine intersubjectivity, data from the mutual assessment underwent the same process. Intersubjectivity (P_t) was thereby measured as a distance between average mutual assessments (AMA) and self-assessment (SA) at a fixed measurement point in time t with the equation $P_t = SA_t - AMA_t$. For the full results of this analysis, please see appendices G, H, and I in the Electronic Supplementary Material.

Additionally, a data quality test was run to determine whether the data collected in the experiment were adequate for identifying the treatment effect. The sessions were compared to see if there was a session effect. This was done by comparing the average icon assessments across sessions, before either group had received the treatment, using the Mann-Whitney U test. As can be seen in Table 5.4, the distributions of the average assessments are not significantly different between sessions in all dimensions and in total. Therefore, it could be concluded that there was no session effect and the data could be used for further analysis.

Table 5.4 Descriptive statistics of average mutual assessments

	Average mutual assessment	Baseline group		Feedback group		SR by icon	U
		mean	sd	mean	sd	p value	p value
Icon 1	**Fresh**	6.48	1.35	6.82	1.61	**0.00**	0.31
	Surprising	5.94	0.96	6.15	1.94	0.13	0.50
	Logical	5.74	1.97	6.10	1.83	0.37	0.58
	Functional	5.30	1.92	5.59	1.86	0.21	0.68
	Understandable	5.28	2.03	5.19	2.14	**0.06**	0.90
	Well-crafted	6.34	1.18	6.22	1.94	**0.09**	0.95
	Total	*35.08*	*7.63*	*36.07*	*8.17*	*0.89*	*0.77*
Icon 2	Fresh	6.15	1.17	5.94	1.76		0.85
	Surprising	5.72	1.15	5.76	2.09		0.79
	Logical	5.96	2.20	6.61	2.37		0.34
	Functional	5.54	1.86	6.24	2.24		0.34
	Understandable	5.76	2.29	6.07	2.27		0.72
	Well-crafted	5.84	1.62	5.99	2.04		0.84
	Total	*34.97*	*8.07*	*36.61*	*9.78*		*0.54*

N_baseline = 20; N_feedback = 20; * $p < 0.05$, ** $p < 0.01$, *** $p < 0.001$ (p-values of a two-sided SR and Mann-Whitney-U test)

It was further determined whether assessments differed between the two icons, i.e., whether one icon received higher average assessments than the other in any of the dimensions. Since the average assessments were collected independently before the treatment, and since the tasks were the same in both sessions and there was no session effect, the sessions can be pooled to obtain more degrees of freedom and increase the power of a Wilcoxon signed-rank test. The results show a significant difference between the icons in the dimension *fresh* at 1% significance level, and in the dimensions *understandable* and *well-crafted* at 10% significance level.

The designs for Icon 1 seemed fresher than the designs for Icon 2, as shown in Fig. 5.3 Both tasks were similar in terms of their application as technical icons and likewise had possible humorous solutions, for example due to ambiguous phrases (the term "shot" can mean "take a picture" or "shoot a gun"). The tasks were obviously not equal in effort. It may have been that participants were biased by already knowing solutions for Icon 2, but not for Icon 1. This leads to some complications in the further analysis, since the tasks are apparently not completely equal and therefore the difference in their assessments may not necessarily show the treatment effect. It should be kept in mind that the results in the dimension *fresh* may not be reliable.

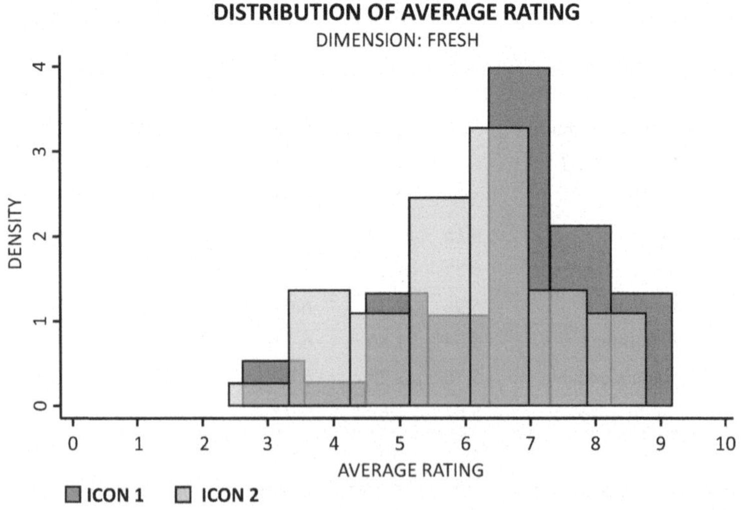

Fig. 5.3 Distribution of the average assessment for fresh

A correlation between the participants' general creativity and the assessments cannot be determined unambiguously. The distributions of the pretest (Williams Creativity Test) and the posttest (Creative Behavior Inventory) give slightly contrasting implications about the overall creativity of the sample. This impression is vaguely supported by the correlation coefficient of −0.05. These results are nevertheless highly insignificant.

To identify a possible correlation between the creativity tests and the assessments, both are further examined via the Spearman correlation test as shown in Table 5.5. The results do not clearly specify which of the creativity tests is more reliable. On closer inspection with a scatterplot, possible correlations between creativity scores from the pre- and posttest and the experimental data can only be seen with a degree of benevolence. The clearest pattern emerges in the dimension *fresh*, for which the Creativity Behavior Inventory has found on the 10% level a significant and marginally stronger negative correlation (rho = − 0.31). There is a lack of comparability of data in this dimension, as described above. Consequently, due to the overall weak correlations, the data from the pre- and posttests were not taken into further consideration.

Table 5.5 Correlations of creativity measurements

	Dimension	Williams Creativity Test		Creative Behavior Inventory	
		rho	p-value	rho	p-value
Icon 1	Fresh	−0.02	0.91	−0.19	0.24
	Surprising	−0.15	0.35	−0.19	0.23
	Logical	0.28	**0.08**	−0.12	0.46
	Functional	0.21	0.20	−0.09	0.58
	Understandable	0.21	0.19	−0.26	0.11
	Well-crafted	0.16	0.32	−0.09	0.60
	Total	*0.13*	*0.41*	*−0.19*	*0.24*
	Self-assessment total	*0.32*	***0.04****	*−0.11*	*0.49*
Icon 2	**Fresh**	0.07	0.68	−0.31	**0.05**
	Surprising	0.08	0.63	−0.21	0.19
	Logical	0.24	0.13	−0.12	0.46
	Functional	0.25	0.13	−0.02	0.88
	Understandable	0.28	**0.08**	−0.07	0.65
	Well-crafted	0.22	0.17	−0.18	0.27
	Total	*0.28*	***0.08***	*−0.18*	*0.25*
	Self-assessment total	*0.11*	*0.52*	*0.06*	*0.72*
	CBI	**−0.05**	**0.75**		

N = 40; * $p < 0.05$, ** $p < 0.01$, *** $p < 0.001$(p-values the Spearman correlation test)

5.3 Findings

This section presents the results of the experiment. The first part demonstrates the general session effects and the correlations between different creativity measures. The second part takes a closer look at intersubjectivity itself. The chapter continues with the statistical results of the found tendencies. The last part investigates how the behavior of the participants changed after receiving feedback for their first icon.

5.3.1 Descriptive Results

To evaluate the main focus of this study, the results of the experimental samples are compared. The variable P_t for the respective intersubjective level is generated from the absolute difference of the self-assessment (SA) minus the average mutual assessment (AMA) for each of the participants. Participants are further separated into over- and underestimators. This means that if their self-assessment is higher than the average mutual assessment they received, they overestimated themselves, and vice versa. Estimators whose self-assessment was the same as their average mutual assessment were rare. These are indicated where necessary.

The baseline and feedback group are compared in total and for the six dimensions separately. The overall statistics in Table 5.6 indicate that participants in both groups misjudge their Icon 1 on the assessment scale (range = 10 points) by around two points with rather high standard deviations. To test whether the groups differ in the precision of the self-evaluation, a Mann-Whitney U test was conducted. The results give no indication of a significant difference except within the dimension *functional*, where the feedback group (mean = 1.38; sd = 1.24) has a lower level of misjudgment than the comparable baseline group (mean = 2.44; sd = 1.74).Observing over- and underestimators further demonstrates the split in the self-evaluation types of the participants within the groups. A similar behavior between the groups can be observed here as well. For example, in both groups, the participants tend to overestimate themselves a fair amount in the dimension *understandable* (baseline = 2.34; feedback = 2.80). In the group of underestimators, the participants misjudge themselves most in the dimension *fresh* (baseline = 2.03; feedback = 2.55).

Table 5.6 Descriptive results

	P_t	Baseline			Feedback			U test
	Dimension	N	mean	sd	N	mean	sd	p value
Icon 1:	Fresh	20	1.61	1.42	20	1.93	1.71	0.92
All	Surprising	20	1.57	0.99	20	2.05	1.48	0.36
	Logical	20	2.12	1.54	20	1.62	1.09	0.33
	Functional	20	2.44	1.74	20	1.38	1.24	**0.04**
	Understandable	20	2.08	1.20	20	2.08	1.58	0.72
	Well-crafted	20	1.63	1.31	20	1.75	1.14	0.61
	Total	20	9.03	4.87	20	7.42	6.04	0.17
Over-estimators	Fresh	8****	1.24	1.34	7****	1.14	1.30	
	Surprising	9	1.28	0.68	7	2.29	1.64	
	Logical	15	2.21	1.60	9	2.32	1.08	
	Functional	15	2.95	1.71	14****	1.58	1.39	
	Understandable	14	2.34	1.15	13****	2.80	1.45	
	Well-crafted	13****	1.58	1.11	12	1.67	1.23	
	Total	13	9.85	4.55	9	9.96	6.75	
Under-estimators	Fresh	11	2.03	1.42	12	2.55	1.72	
	Surprising	11	1.81	1.17	13	1.93	1.45	
	Logical	5	1.82	1.45	11	1.05	0.71	
	Functional	5	0.92	0.53	5	1.12	0.54	
	Understandable	6	1.45	1.16	5	1.02	0.52	
	Well-crafted	6	2.02	1.69	8	1.85	1.04	
	Total	7	7.51	5.44	10	5.88	4.61	

N_baseline = 20; N_feedback = 20; * $p < 0.05$, ** $p < 0.01$, *** $p < 0.001$ (p-values of a two-sided Mann-Whitney U test), **** correct estimations excluded

Looking at the different shares of estimations over both groups, it is noticeable that the participants generally overestimate themselves more often in the dimensions *functional, understandable,* and *well-crafted,* while they underestimated themselves more often in the dimensions *fresh* and *surprising.* Only in the dimension of *logical* does there seem to be a difference between the baseline and the feedback group in terms of over- and underestimation tendencies.

To determine if there is any general significant difference in the shares of over- and underestimators, a binominal test was conducted jointly for Icon 1 as shown in Table 5.7. The tendency to overestimate oneself is highly significant only in the dimensions *functional* ($p = 0.003$) and *understandable* ($p = 0.01$). For the other dimensions, the null hypothesis of equal distributions between over- and underestimators in the baseline and feedback group cannot be rejected.

Table 5.7 Sample composition for overestimators (O) and underestimators (U)

	Dimensions	Over-estimator	Under-estimator	k > = O	K < = O	K < = U or k > = O
		N	N	p	p	p
Icon 1	Fresh	15	23	0.93	0.13	0.26
	Surprising	16	24	0.92	0.13	0.27
	Logical	24	16	0.13	0.92	0.27
	Functional	29	10	**0.002****	1.00	**0.003****
	Understandable	27	11	**0.007****	1.00	**0.01***
	Well-crafted	25	14	**0.05**	0.97	0.11
	Total	21	17	0.31	0.79	0.63

* $p < 0.05$, ** $p < 0.01$, *** $p < 0.001$ (p-values of a one and two-sided binomial test); H0: Shares $\neq 0.5$

5.3.2 Hypothesis 1: Precision of Self-assessment

To begin hypothesis testing, the treatment effect regarding the precision of self-assessment was examined. Hypothesis 1 stated that receiving feedback on the creation would be associated with better accuracy in self-assessment compared to average mutual assessments in the future. A Mann-Whitney U test comparing the two sessions with respect to the differences in the intersubjective level P_2 of the Icon 2, did not find any significant differences between the baseline and feedback group, as shown in Table 5.8.

Table 5.8 Mann-Whitney U test comparing the intersubjective levels P_2 of Icon 2

	Dimension	Baseline		Feedback		U
		mean	sd	mean	sd	p value
P_2 (Icon 2)	Fresh	1.58	1.27	1.83	1.38	0.59
	Surprising	1.57	1.16	1.59	1.47	0.65
	Logical	1.90	1.68	1.65	1.19	0.99
	Functional	1.94	1.72	1.55	1.06	0.90
	Understandable	1.68	1.59	1.64	0.83	0.33
	Well-crafted	2.13	1.53	1.74	1.36	0.45
	Total	8.69	6.00	7.78	5.07	0.63
$\Delta P = P_1 - P_2$	Fresh	0.03	1.86	0.10	2.52	0.96
	Surprising	−0.00	1.37	0.47	2.25	0.43
	Logical	0.21	2.16	−0.03	1.57	0.46
	Functional	0.51	1.80	−0.16	1.54	0.23
	Understandable	0.40	1.73	0.44	1.86	0.98
	Well-crafted	−0.50	1.71	0.00	1.98	0.40
	Total	0.34	5.85	−0.37	7.72	0.76

N_baseline = 20; N_feedback = 20; $^{*}\ p < 0.05$, $^{**}\ p < 0.01$, $^{***}\ p < 0.001$ (p-values of a two-sided Mann-Whitney U test)

Further, a Wilcoxon signed-rank test compared the intersubjective levels P_t of the two icons within the feedback group, shown in Table 5.9. Again, no significant differences were found.

An exception is the dimension *understandable* in the subsample of overestimators, where significantly lower self-assessments were determined for Icon 2. Nevertheless, Hypothesis 1 must be rejected with regard to the overall results: Providing feedback about the creation does not lead to a more precise self-evaluation.

Table 5.9 Wilcoxon signed-rank test comparing intersubjective levels P_t of Icons 1 and 2

	Feedback group		Icon 1		Icon 2		SR
	P_t	N	mean	sd	mean	sd	p value
Icon 1:	Fresh	20	1.93	1.71	1.83	1.38	0.67
All	Surprising	20	2.05	1.48	1.59	1.47	0.26
	Logical	20	1.62	1.09	1.65	1.19	0.89
	Functional	20	1.38	1.24	1.55	1.06	0.63
	Understandable	20	2.08	1.58	1.64	0.83	0.39
	Well-crafted	20	1.75	1.14	1.74	1.36	0.96
	Total	20	7.42	6.04	7.78	5.07	0.83
Over	Fresh	7	1.14	1.30	1.36	0.69	0.28
	Surprising	7	2.29	1.64	1.79	2.02	0.47
	Logical	9	2.32	1.08	1.63	1.17	0.13
	Functional	14	1.58	1.39	1.65	1.14	0.89
	Understandable	13	2.80	1.45	1.57	0.86	**0.02**
	Well-crafted	12	1.67	1.23	2.00	1.57	0.62
	Total	9	9.96	6.75	9.30	6.53	0.73
Under	Fresh	12	2.55	1.72	1.91	1.53	0.30
	Surprising	13	1.93	1.45	1.48	1.17	0.38
	Logical	11	1.05	0.71	1.65	1.25	0.15
	Functional	5	1.12	0.54	1.04	0.72	0.88
	Understandable	5	1.02	0.52	1.64	0.96	0.63
	Well-crafted	8	1.85	1.04	1.36	0.95	0.38
	Total	10	5.88	4.61	6.00	2.94	0.83

N = 40; * $p < 0.05$, ** $p < 0.01$, *** $p < 0.001$ (p-values of a Wilcoxon signed-rank test of icons 1 and 2)

5.3.3 Hypothesis 2: Movement of Self-assessments

Hypothesis 2 examines the direction of the movement of participants' self-evaluations after feedback. One would intuitively assume that participants who receive feedback will adjust their behavior, e.g., by overcompensating. This means that participants who initially overestimated themselves will adapt their self-assessments downward for Icon 2, and participants who initially underestimated themselves will adapt their self-assessments upward to the average mutual assessment.

The next step takes a closer look at the pure movement behavior of the participants. Some change their type from overestimating to underestimating, and vice versa. The no-feedback group changed its type in 20–45% of cases, while the group with feedback changed much more frequently, between 35% and 65% depending on the dimension. A Fisher's exact test was used to find out whether these descriptive differences between the groups are significant. The results show that, in the dimensions *functional* (baseline = 0.20; feedback = 0.60) and *understandable* (baseline = 0.20; feedback = 0.65), participants in the feedback group were significantly more often willing to change their self-assessment.

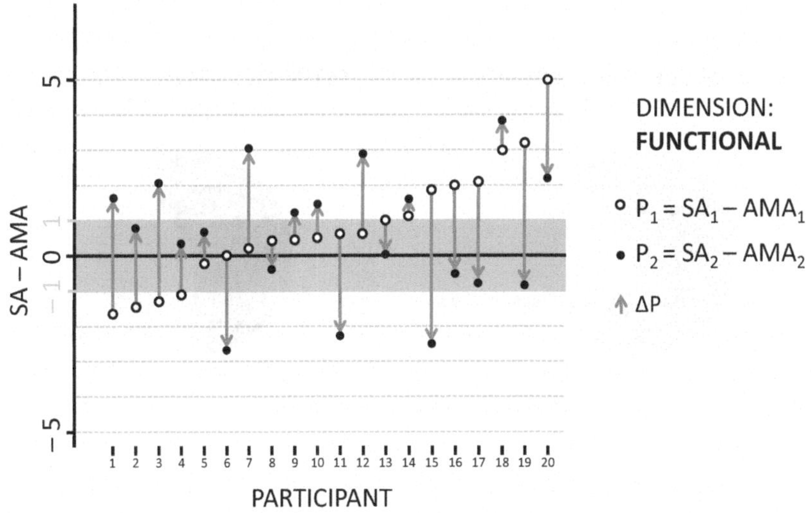

Fig. 5.4 Movement of self-assessment in the dimension functional

To shed more light on movement in self-assessments, the two particularly significant dimensions, *functional* and *understandable*, were examined in more detail. As demonstrated in Fig. 5.4, in the dimension *functional*, 65% of participants in the feedback group moved their self-assessment in the direction of the feedback—in many cases beyond it and over a large range of several points. This did not make the self-assessment any more precise, as one might have expected. Of particular note here are two very precise estimates for Icon 1 from participants who moved away considerably from their initially precise self-assessment when it came to Icon 2, despite having received feedback confirming the accuracy of their original estimate.

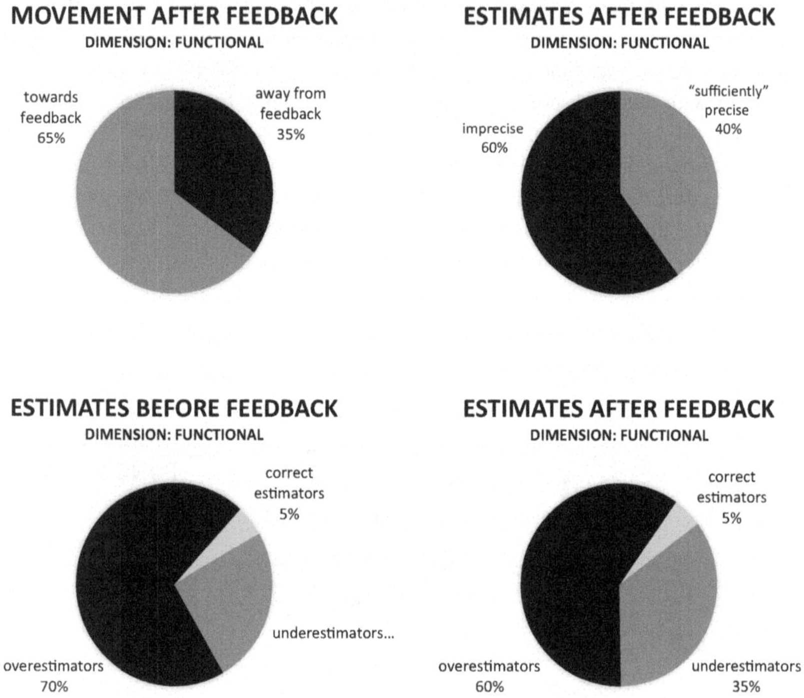

Fig. 5.5 Behavior with feedback in the dimension functional

The significant movement of self-estimation after feedback in the dimension *functional* still comes with a large number of imprecise estimates of 60% after feedback, as Fig. 5.5 demonstrates. The strong change between over- and underestimators is likewise evident in the comparison of the estimates before and after feedback. The low number of correct estimators remains the same at 5%, while the number of overestimators decreases from 70% to 60% and the number of underestimators increases from 25% to 35%. As shown in Fig. 5.4, many participants switch types due to the considerably large value change in self-assessment.

The strong movement in self-assessment after feedback becomes even more evident in the dimension *understandable*, as demonstrated in Fig. 5.6. Here, the movement and the resulting change between over- and underestimators is even more pronounced. Two accurate estimators move away from the feedback significantly, despite confirmation of their correct estimate. In contrast, two quite imprecise estimators hardly change their self-assessment after feedback, and even move in the "wrong" direction, away from the feedback.

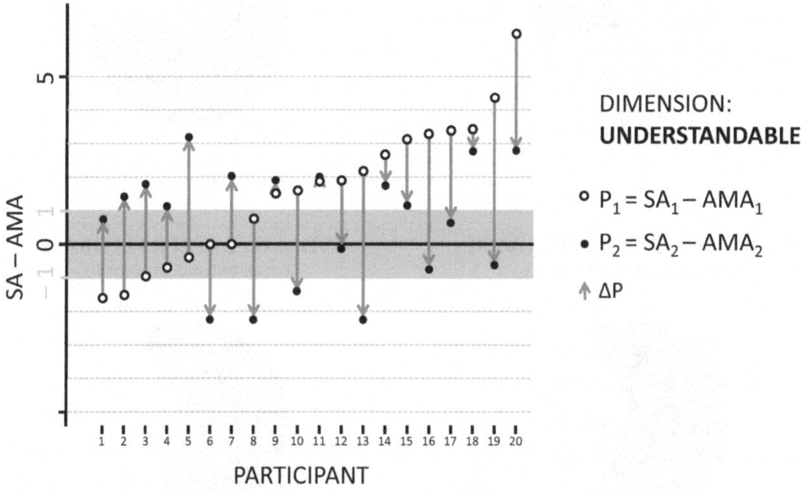

Fig. 5.6 Movement of self-assessment in the dimension understandable

In the dimension *understandable*, the movement towards the feedback is very high, at 80%, as can be seen in Fig. 5.7. In contrast to *functional*, this dimension additionally includes a participant who has not changed their self-assessment at all. The imprecise estimates after feedback of 75% stay on the highest level and demonstrate an even stronger change between over- and underestimators than in the dimension *functional,* as described above. The correct estimators decrease from 10% to 5% after feedback, which serves as another indication for the rejection of Hypothesis 1 about precise estimations. The distribution of types remains mostly the same; underestimators increase after feedback from 25% to 30% and overestimators stay at 65% after feedback. It is noticeable that in most cases a switch of type between over- and underestimator occurred.

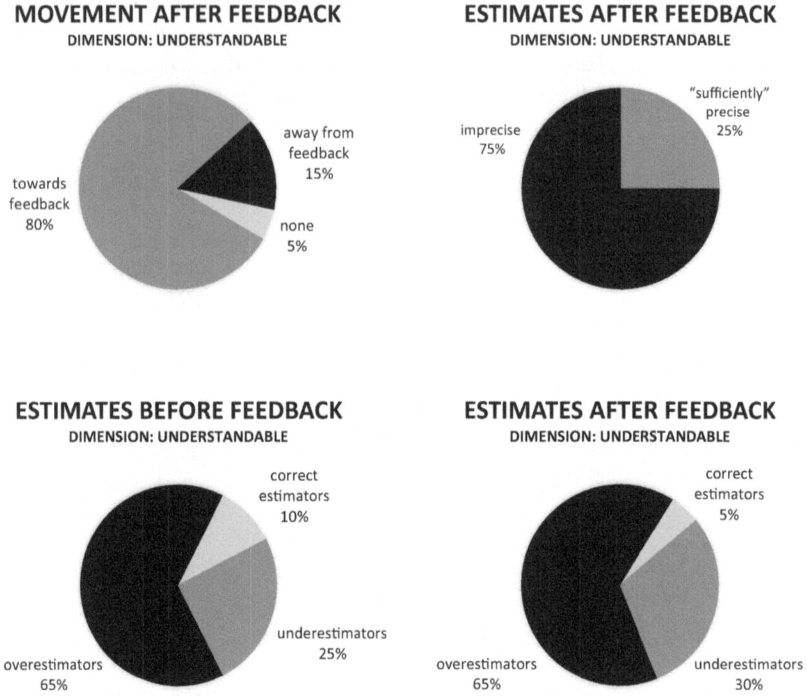

Fig. 5.7 Behavior with feedback in the dimension understandable

As mentioned earlier, participants behaved quite irrationally: Participants who performed well in the assessment of Icon 1 appear to be very imprecise in their assessment after receiving the feedback. It is notable that those participants did not much change the value of their self-assessment for Icon 2. For example, one participant was "sufficiently precise" in self-assessing Icon 1 (located in the given one-point interval [AMA − 1, AMA + 1]) and earned the precision bonus. It seems that this participant decided not to adjust the self-assessment regarding the design quality of Icon 2 and just gave themself the same rating, naively thinking that they would get the bonus again. It may likewise be that the new conditions of a second task were ignored for other reasons, such as irritation or discomfort from unexpected feedback.

5.3.4 Summary of Results

Intersubjectivity (P_t) was measured in the laboratory experiment as a distance between average mutual assessments (AMA) and self-assessment (SA) at a fixed measurement point in time t with the equation $P_t = SA_t - AMA_t$. This newly developed measurement was applied to a variety of criteria such as creativity tests and assessment dimensions. It was found that several creativity tests do not correlate with intersubjectivity. It can therefore be deduced that intersubjectivity is unrelated to creativity.

The investigation of the six assessment dimensions *fresh, surprising, logical, functional, understandable,* and *well-crafted* demonstrates that over- and underestimation is dependent on the dimension. Participants' tendency to underestimate themselves is associated with the dimension *fresh*, while overestimation is associated with the dimension *understandable.* Despite the tendency to overestimate, however, *understandable* is the dimension where the most movement in self-assessment can be observed. When confronted with feedback on the understandability of their creation, participants were most likely to change their self-assessment. In the dimension *understandable,* 80% of participants moved their self-assessment towards the feedback. Moreover, participants changed their type from over- to underestimator (or vice versa) the most in the dimension *understandable.* These findings speak for a learning effect, albeit with a significant limitation: The movement and the changes between over- and underestimators did not lead to more precise self-assessments. Despite all movements, the average self-assessment actually remained the same. Intersubjectivity, understood as an aligning of self-assessments with feedback, did not increase. Participants predominantly continued to assess themselves irrationally after feedback. The laboratory experiment demonstrated that providing feedback about the understandability of the creation does not lead to a more precise self-assessment in participants and thus does not foster overall intersubjectivity.

5.4 Discussion

The experiment in Study III dealt with a wide range of creativity assessments. This was an opportunity to find orientation in the unsettled research field of the measurement and learning of intersubjectivity: It was found that intersubjectivity can be measured between external (or mutual) assessments and self-assessment. Thereby, the question of the understandability of the creation was identified as key for moving the self-assessments of co-creators. It can, however, be stated that no significant learning effects on intersubjectivity can be generated within the short period of time of an experiment or one workshop. This leads to the assumption that intersubjectivity is a trait rather than a learnable skill, and is unrelated to the creativity of co-creators. These implications contribute to open innovation practice and to the learning theory on intersubjectivity.

5.4.1 From a Research Perspective

Intersubjectivity can be measured by the distance between average mutual (or external) assessments and self-assessment

The developed measurements for intersubjectivity (P_t) as a distance between average mutual (or external) assessments (AMA) and self-assessment (SA) at a fixed measurement point in time t with the equation $P_t = SA_t - AMA_t$ can determine movements in assessments well. This significantly extends the recommendations of Ehrkirch and Matsumae (2024) for measuring intersubjectivity inside co-creative groups to a new perspective focused on the users. This new approach gives practitioners a hands-on way of determining the market potential of an idea beyond a single co-creator. It might be interesting to investigate more possibilities to determine the variable P in one step without elaborative second tasks or external assessments.

Movement in co-creator self-assessments depends on the dimension

This study provides some insights into how to deal with intersubjectivity. Just as overconfidence depends on the circumstances (Moore & Healy, 2008; Pallier et al., 2002), it was found that over- and underestimation are dependent on the dimension. When participants underestimate themselves, they tend to do so in the dimension *fresh*. This seems logical, because the creation is naturally not new for the creator, although it is for the other participants. On the other hand, when participants overestimate themselves, they tend to do that in the dimension *understandable*. This seems similarly logical, because a creator surely understands their own work better than others. When participants changed their estimation after feedback (from over- to underestimation or vice versa), it was in the dimension *understandable*. Co-creators are most likely to try and change their self-assessment when confronted with the understandability of their creation, although this does not inevitably lead to more precise estimates. The average self-assessment actually remained the same after feedback, despite strong movements in self-assessments. This may, however, be a first indication that learning effects might exist for intersubjectivity after all.

Co-creators do not learn intersubjectivity through immediate feedback

The laboratory experiment found that feedback did not lead to any significant overall learning effect in terms of intersubjectivity. At first glance, this directly confirms researchers who found that feedback does not induce learning and that intersubjectivity remains a static personal trait (Kruger & Dunning, 1999; Pallier et al., 2002; Schlösser et al., 2013). Nevertheless, there was a strong movement of self-assessments after feedback on *understandability*, even if it did not lead to higher estimation precision or meaningful learning. The participants still behaved considerably irrationally after feedback. In cases where underestimators corrected their self-assessments upwards beyond the feedback, the better-than-average effect (Alicke & Govorun, 2005) could be assumed as a reason. Yet this would not fully explain the irrational self-assessment behavior. One reason for this might be the short time period with only one round of feedback, or the relatively small number of participants. It could be that the learning effects simply take too long to develop for it to be possible to find them in a single workshop (Krajc & Ortmann, 2008; Mayo et al., 2012; Murphy, 2017), and that the feedback in some dimensions feels too unexpected and uncomfortable to generate learning (Mezirow, 1991). Neither case—subjectivity as either a trait or a skill that can only be learned with effort and time—is compatible with the usually rather short-term integration of co-creators in open innovation projects. In the context of a workshop, it is therefore necessary to work with the level of intersubjectivity that co-creators bring with them. This makes intersubjectivity relevant as a selection criterion for co-creators.

In open innovation practice, feedback to co-creators is considered essential for their learning (Roth et al., 2017). It might be of great interest to further investigate the exact circumstances of the irrational behavior after feedback that occurred in this experiment. The self-assessment procedures in following investigations could be adapted to avoid effects like naïve behavior or unwanted learning. The task design could moreover be developed to suit tasks that already have data for comparison, to avoid uncertainties.

5.4.2 From a Managerial Perspective

Intersubjectivity is a trait, unrelated to creativity

It is important for practitioners to know that no significant learning effects for intersubjectivity can be generated within a short time, such as in a laboratory experiment or one workshop. Intersubjectivity may therefore be considered as a static trait (Kruger & Dunning, 1999; Pallier et al., 2002; Schlösser et al., 2013) and not a learnable skill (Krajc & Ortmann, 2008; Mayo et al., 2012; Murphy, 2017). Accordingly, if organizers want innovative ideas to have more than just individual potential, they are dependent in intersubjectivity as a trait. Co-creators may already bring this trait with them or it may be identified during the workshop.

When selecting co-creators, intersubjectivity could be seen in connection with the creativity of co-creators, as this concept originates from creativity research (Chong, 2013). It seems logical to attribute intersubjectivity to creative consumers (P. Berthon et al., 2011) or, more generally, to attribute intersubjectivity to creativity as a selection criterion for co-creators (Bogers et al., 2017). The laboratory experiment demonstrated that there is no correlation between the creativity of co-creators and their intersubjectivity. Intersubjectivity may therefore be considered as an independent trait, unrelated to creativity.

Understandability is the key dimension for moving self-assessments

Not surprisingly, feedback on understandability stimulates co-creators the most to change their self-assessment. This is probably because it is the dimension closest to the definition of intersubjectivity as "shared understanding" (Burford et al., 2013; Cash et al., 2017; Shapin, 2017; Talamo & Pozzi, 2011). The question of a creation's understandability may be a main driver for the personal development of co-creators' intersubjectivity. Overestimators gave significantly lower self-assessments after feedback on understandability, and 80% of participants then moved their self-assessment towards the feedback. These results on moving self-assessments could be a first step to helping organizations co-create more efficiently. They could assess the market potential and self-assessment skills of co-creators in advance, when asking potential co-creators about the understandability of their creation, and thus encourage them to consider the perspective of other users. This approach could counteract risky evaluation biases that inhibit the remarkable potential of creative users and could be further investigated.

5.4.3 Summary of Findings

This laboratory experiment found that intersubjectivity is a trait in itself, unrelated to creativity. As a result, it may be considered as an independent selection criterion for co-creators. To determine intersubjectivity, the present study contributes to theory an intersubjectivity measurement between external (or mutual) assessments and self-assessment. This measurement method made it possible to test a variety of assessment dimensions. Understandability of the creation was identified as the key dimension for moving self-assessments by co-creators, and could be subject to more detailed investigation. The movement in self-assessment does not, however, lead to more precision in self-assessment, as co-creators react irrationally to feedback. No significant overall learning effect from feedback in terms of intersubjectivity could be found. Therefore, selecting co-creators by their intersubjective traits becomes even more relevant.

YOUR ITEMS FROM STUDY III

- Intersubjectivity is a trait in itself, unrelated to creativity.
- Intersubjectivity can be measured between external (or mutual) assessments and self-assessment.
- Understandability is the key dimension for moving self-assessments.
- Co-creators react irrationally to feedback.

6 Study IV: Experimenting with Intersubjectivity in the Field

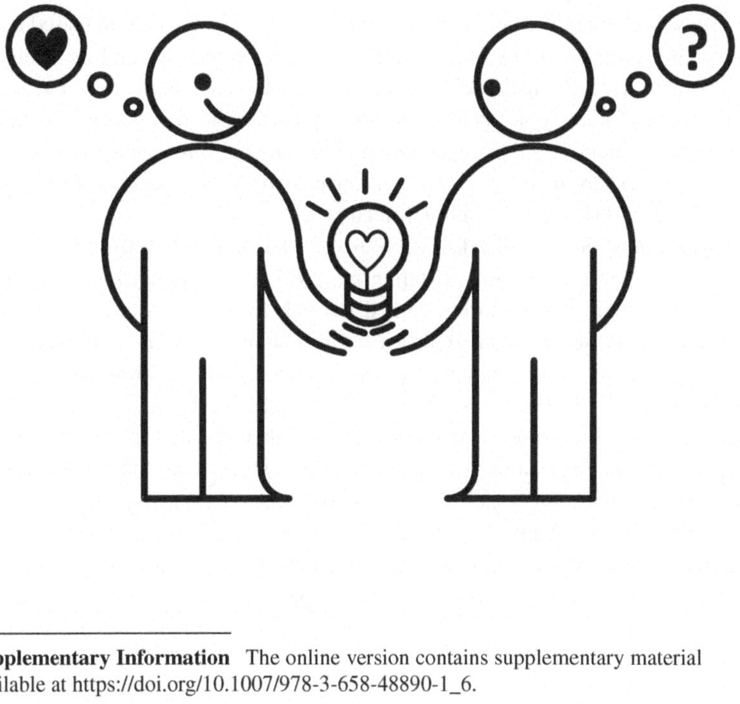

Supplementary Information The online version contains supplementary material available at https://doi.org/10.1007/978-3-658-48890-1_6.

M. Oßwald, *When Co-Creation Leads to Love*, Markt- und Unternehmensentwicklung Markets and Organisations,
https://doi.org/10.1007/978-3-658-48890-1_6

Many co-creators continue to self-assess irrationally with feedback, and struggle or even fail to develop intersubjectivity. Since intersubjectivity may be essential for the efficiency of open innovation, strategies need to be found to work with more intersubjective co-creators in the future, either by training or by identifying them. Understandability of the creation may be a key dimension for the development of intersubjectivity in co-creators. With two field quasi-experiments, Study IV[1] intends to transfer the previous findings into open innovation practice. In this chapter, two differently composed workshop groups and a total of 20 co-creators are studied for their behavior regarding intersubjectivity to identify ways of learning intersubjectivity or find intersubjective co-creators.

6.1 Research Objective

When selecting suitable co-creators for innovation processes with increased quality, innovating organizations need to understand the boundaries and mechanisms of intersubjectivity. Realistic self-assessment through intersubjectivity paves the way for more efficiency in open innovation. According to the theory, it is undecided whether intersubjectivity is a measurable personal trait that should be used as a selection criterion for co-creators in open innovation processes, or if it is a skill that can be learned, e.g., through feedback.

In open innovation, feedback is seen as essential to foster learning processes for a variety of co-creator skills (Roth et al., 2017). Yet it is not known if intersubjectivity is a skill that can be learned through feedback. Several researchers and practitioners indicate that, with a certain amount of effort, task repetition, financial incentives, and feedback, learning effects can be produced in self-assessment (Krajc & Ortmann, 2008; Murphy, 2017). Apart from the effort, learning depends on gender and takes time, which is needed to translate feedback into self-awareness and subsequent learning (Mayo et al., 2012). Moreover, unexpected feedback outcomes may result in an unpleasant experience, which can inhibit learning effects (Mezirow, 1991). It may well be that learning intersubjectivity takes too long and requires too much effort to reasonably engage in learning processes in innovation co-creation projects.

[1] Study IV is based on an unpublished working paper (Oßwald, 2020) presented at the 2020 research colloquium Innovation and Value Creation in Nuremberg (Germany) and another unpublished working paper (Oßwald, 2024) presented at the 2024 research colloquium Innovation and Value Creation in Erfurt (Germany).

Intersubjectivity might be seen as unlearnable because it is too difficult to learn in the context of open innovation. Other researchers do not believe that intersubjectivity can be learned at all and consider it to be a static trait. For example, the Dunning-Kruger test (Kruger & Dunning, 1999) identifies self-assessments in four static performance groups that are defined by external assessment. The self-assessment is similarly high across all four performance groups, while the actual, externally assessed performance increases from group to group. This means that low performers asses themselves as highly as high performers do. The static nature of performance groups was later supported by another experiment that relied on external feedback (Schlösser et al., 2013). Other experiments, such as on the overconfidence effect (Pallier et al., 2002) identified self-confidence (which leads to overestimation) as a trait that relies in part on cognitive ability. A subsequent study on the topic found that overestimating oneself is context-dependent and that people usually tend to overestimate their ability (Moore & Healy, 2008).

The laboratory experiment in Study III produced some remarkable insights about learning intersubjectivity in an open innovation context. Evidence was found to support the theory that intersubjectivity is problematic or impossible to learn through feedback (Krajc & Ortmann, 2008; Kruger & Dunning, 1999; Maya et al., 2012; Schlösser et al., 2013). An intersubjectivity measurement between a co-creator and users was additionally introduced. The previous laboratory experiment left unanswered some questions that should be clarified, such as the strong movement towards and beyond the feedback. Other irrational behavior, such as precise estimators moving away from the feedback, should be further investigated. It remained unclear whether there were any undesired side effects, for example, through the different, nonequivalent tasks. The most crucial question is to what extent the preceding findings can be transferred to open innovation practice. Laboratory experiments, despite their high internal validity, are often too contrived and difficult to compare with professional practice due to the participation of students (Gordon et al., 1986). This study is dedicated to the practical application of the preceding findings and is designed to add external validity and clarify missing points. To capture the whole picture of the learning of intersubjectivity in an open innovation context, two field quasi-experiments based on the previous study are now presented.

The previous study tested a broad range of different measures for their suitability for learning intersubjectivity. These were creativity tests like the other-rated William's Creativity Test Part A (Williams, 1980) and the self-rated Creative Behavior Inventory (Hocevar, 1980). Moreover, the six dimensions *fresh, surprising, logical, functional, understandable,* and *well-crafted* from the Creative Product Semantic Scale (O'Quin & Besemer, 1989) were investigated. Upon investigation, the dimension *understandable* could be defined as key dimension for possibly learning intersubjectivity. With the question of the understandability of their creation, co-creators can be stimulated to move their self-assessment towards feedback and counter typical overestimation. Nevertheless, the mean distances to feedback remained quite similar. Despite a lot of movement, intersubjectivity as an aligning of self-assessments with feedback could not be increased. It would be relevant to know definitively whether there are substantial learning effects in co-creators or not. This would determine whether this is a skill to be encouraged through feedback on understandability or a trait to be used from the start as a selection criterion for co-creators. This chapter consequently investigates the following research question:

RQ IV: Do co-creators learn intersubjectivity through feedback about the understandability of their creation?

6.2 Research Design: Field Quasi-Experiment

To investigate evaluation biases in greater depth, this study aims to explore whether more realistic estimation can be trained by feedback about the understandability of the creations. To answer the research question and to complement the previous laboratory experiment, two field quasi-experiments with a one-group pretest-posttest design (O_1-X-O_2) were conducted during separate co-creation workshops. The method was chosen to gain internal validity in combination with external validity without overly influencing the "real life" (Campbell & Stanley, 1966; Grant & Wall, 2009) and thereby supporting generalizability with a maximum of realism (Gordon et al., 1986). This approach is particularly suitable for facilitating collaboration with practitioners and using context to explain conflicting findings (Grant & Wall, 2009), such as the irrational impact of feedback on self-assessment.

6.2.1 Experimental Procedure

The experimental design of this study aims to reflect common co-creation settings such as workshops in creative spaces. In order to establish a strong reference to open innovation practice, both field quasi-experiments were conducted in two co-creation workshops in the Leistungszentrum Elektroniksysteme (LZE)[2], a technology transfer institution in Erlangen (Germany). The experimental tasks in the workshops were part of and contributed to business development projects conducted by LZE. The topic of the first workshop was to find ideas for a consumer application for a portable X-ray device, while the second workshop aimed to find ideas for a consumer application for a new display technology. The experiments took place in two typical innovation co-creation workshops in different group compositions with around 10 participants each. The goal was to use the different compositions and the collaboration modes (established/newly composed, self-selected/selected) to draw conclusions about selecting co-creators for more intersubjectivity towards users.

The first workshop group had a homogeneous composition of male participants from an engineering environment and with high expertise in the technological field. The group had been established by self-selection in the context of LZE cooperation partners. At the time of the field quasi-experiment, the group had already held several similar innovation and co-creation workshops on the same topic. This workshop group represented an actual, established practice of innovation co-creation.

The second workshop group had a diverse composition of co-creators specifically selected for one innovation co-creation workshop. Participants were chosen using a variety of selection criteria, such as male/female, age, and professional backgrounds in terms of closeness to consumer market, innovativeness, and scholar/practitioner. Just under half of the participants were already familiar with the new display technology involved in the task. This diverse group was purposely composed as differently as possible from the homogeneous group in order to draw conclusions on co-creator selection criteria and their implementation. An overview of the workshops is given in Table 6.1.

[2] www.lze.bayern

Table 6.1 Overview of experimental workshops

OVERVIEW OF EXPERIMENTAL WORKSHOPS		
	HOMOGENEOUS GROUP	DIVERSE GROUP
TASK	Consumer application for portable X-ray device	Consumer application for new display technology
PARTICIPANTS	11 (11 m / age 26–46)	9 (5 m, 4 f / age 25–58)
CHARACTERISTICS	100% from engineering environment / 77% X-ray technology experts	different professional backgrounds (closeness to consumer market, innovativeness, scholar/practitioner) / 44% familiar with new display technology
COLLABORATION MODE	Established group, part of workshop series, self-selected co-creators	Newly composed group for one workshop, selected co-creators
WORKSHOP MODE	Video Conference 1	Video Conference 2
EXPERIMENTAL PROCEDURE	Two separate runs of the six stages of the experimental procedure	

The workshops were complemented with external assessment from the open innovation lab JOSEPHS in Nuremberg[3], which is associated with LZE. Altogether, 100 random visitors (50 per workshop group) served as user experts for the external assessments (Haller et al., 2017). This was done to determine realistic performance groups for the Dunning-Kruger test (Schlösser et al., 2013).

6.2.1.1 Experimental Stages

The present field quasi-experiments were based on the experimental design of the Dunning-Kruger's lab test design variation with feedback (Schlösser et al., 2013). The procedure provides a sound basis for demonstrating intersubjectivity by identifying overestimators, correct estimators, and underestimators in self-assessment and dividing them into four performance groups that are defined by external feedback. The structure of the original three-stage experimental structure performed in two rounds was adapted to a one-group pretest-posttest design (O_1-X-O_2) with six stages, as shown in Fig. 6.1. The details of the stages are presented in the following sections.

[3] http://www.josephs-innovation.de

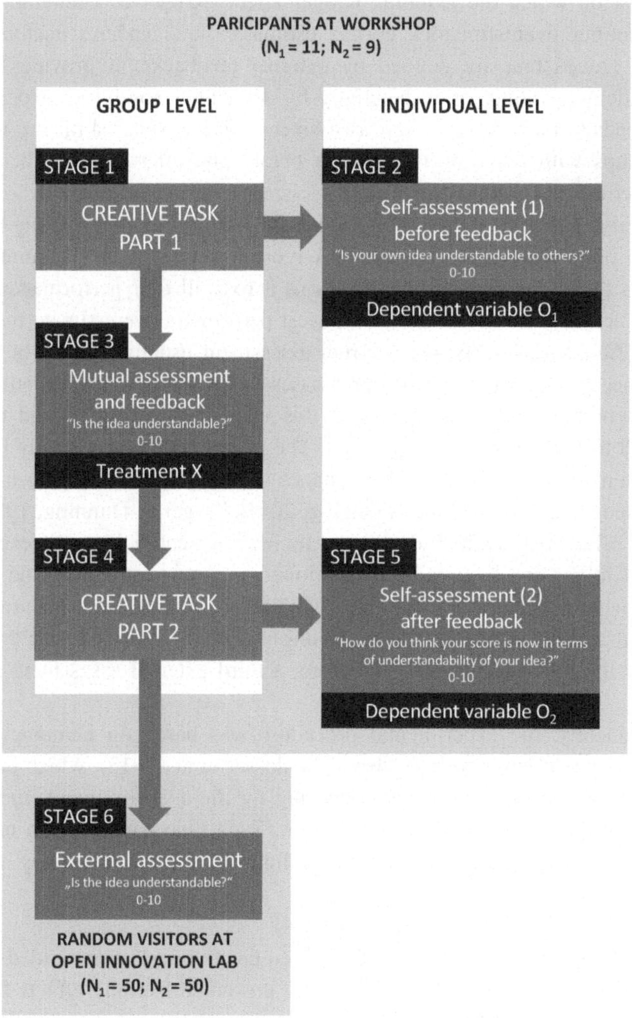

Fig. 6.1 Structure of the field quasi-experiments. (Author's illustration)

The test on which the Dunning-Kruger effect (Kruger & Dunning, 1999) is based identifies overestimators, correct estimators, and underestimators in performance groups that are defined by external feedback[4]. It provides an ideal basis for demonstrating intersubjectivity by describing how more expertise in a domain leads to more realistic self-assessments. Participants' skills are identified in four steps with two self-assessments before and after a task. These scores are then compared with an external assessment, which is given by experts in the respective field and staged into performance groups by determining the quartiles from one (bottom) to four (top). A typical pattern of the Dunning-Kruger test shows fairly consistent self-estimations across all four performance groups, while the actual score increases. The lowest performers overestimate themselves the most. Self-assessments and external assessment usually overlap in the third performance group, where participants assess themselves most realistically and can be identified very conveniently in this way. Top performers, on the other hand, tend to underestimate themselves. The phenomenon has already been recognized in many different skills, for instance in humor, grammar, games, medical lab knowledge, and firearm use (Dunning, 2011; Kruger & Dunning, 1999). This approach offers two major advantages for the present field quasi-experiment. First, it identifies and focuses on overestimators, correct estimators and underestimators, which provides comparability with the laboratory experiment and adds the second advantage that has been missing so far: external and thus "real" validation of the self-assessments. Therefore, a third external assessment step was added.

Consequently, the experimental procedure was based on Dunning-Kruger's lab test design variation with feedback (Schlösser et al., 2013), which previously took place in several sessions. Considering the field environment, the process was merged into a single workshop session. Such time condensation minimizes potential confounding threats to internal validity (Campbell & Stanley, 1966).

6.2.1.1.1 Creative Task (Stages 1 and 4)

For the solving of a co-creation task, one co-creative task was divided into two sequential steps for stages 1 and 4 to avoid unwanted learning effects from task repetition or incomparable tasks. The tasks were to be completed in two steps, before and after the feedback, and to be solved on an individual level rather than in the group.

---

[4] The Dunning-Kruger effect is often misinterpreted in popular literature as only concerning unskilled people's overestimation of themselves. This thesis uses the underlying test of the effect for determining and displaying overestimators, correct estimators, and underestimators.

The tasks had to be designed in such a way that participants could act as experts when assessing them in the mutual assessments. This is possible because co-creators combine the roles of creator and potential user in one person. Such tasks should be intuitive and self-explanatory (Greve et al., 2016), and easy to learn to mitigate overconfidence biases (Moore & Healy, 2008). With this in mind, the use of icons was identified as an appropriate medium for task solving in this experiment. Icons are an internationally standardized form of communication beyond language. They have become an integral part of people's everyday lives, be it in the design of computer program icons or emoticons such as the smiley face (Abdullah & Hübner, 2005). Icons can be used to transfer information independent of language and as quickly as possible, thus serving as a low-barrier means of communication. Their use is an easy way to convey information, such as ideas, regardless of design skills (Urban, 1995). The simple form of communication through icons is ideal for communication between the two roles of creator and user.

Moreover, a lack of drawing talent should not impact the results, so the workshop used simple digital sketch board templates on the platform Padlet[5]. The tasks in the present laboratory experiment were about finding suitable icons or other images from the Padlet database that would represent the application idea. With this constrained task approach, workshop participants could create appealing designs with as little effort and design knowledge as possible (Dahl & Moreau, 2007; Greve et al., 2016). In preparation, all workshop participants were briefed in person prior to the workshop. They were given their personal sketch board template with an anonymized identification number in advance to familiarize themselves with the tool. On the template, there were already playful design instructions and suggestions (Gerve et al., 2016) that had been worked out with the project leaders at LZE. The sketch boards had integrated questionnaires for surveying the general characteristics of participants such as age, technological expertise, profession, their self-assessments for stages 2 and 5, and whether they changed their design after feedback. The sketch board templates can be found in Appendix J in the Electronic Supplementary Material for the homogeneous workshop group and in Appendix K in the Electronic Supplementary Material for the diverse workshop group.

[5] www.padlet.com

The creative task in both workshops was to illustrate a new consumer application for a high-tech device in two sequential steps: first, to describe an application field, and second, to demonstrate the use of the device with appropriate icons or pictures from the Padlet database. In Stage 4, workshop participants were given the opportunity to revise their individual sketch boards from Stage 1 in the second part of the task, based on the mutual assessment feedback.

6.2.1.1.2 Self-assessment (Stages 2 and 5)

The workshop participants' individual self-assessments were surveyed before the mutual assessment and feedback, and after the second part of the task. After processing a first version of their idea in Task 1, participants were asked for their self-assessment before feedback with the question: "*Is your idea understandable to others?*" The specific question of understandability was derived from the results of the laboratory experiment in Study III. The question dimension emerged primarily from the investigation of the Creative Product Semantic Scale (O'Quin & Besemer, 1989). It was found that this dimension motivates most movement in self-assessments, especially towards feedback. Likewise, this is the dimension closest to the definition of intersubjectivity as "shared understanding" (Burford et al., 2013; Cash et al., 2017; Shapin, 2017; Talamo & Pozzi, 2011).

The assessment was conducted with the "projective technique" of asking participants to identify which outcome others would prefer (Fisher, 1993). It was surveyed with the same Likert scale as in the Dunning-Kruger test and the preceding laboratory experiment for comparability, using ratings of 0–10 (0 = very poorly; 10 = very well) to measure the dependent variable O_1. Upon completion of the second part of the task, participants were asked to rate themselves again in Step 5 to generate their second self-assessment after feedback ("*How understandable is your idea to others now?*") on a scale of 0–10 to measure the dependent variable O_2.

6.2.1.1.3 Mutual Assessment Feedback (Stage 3)

Stage 3 of mutual assessment through feedback served as Treatment X: All sketch boards were presented anonymously to the group. Workshop participants rated each other with the online voting tool Mentimeter[6] ("*How well do you understand the ideas shown?*") on a scale of 0–10, to generate the score for mutual feedback for rapid identification of possible learning effects. Since workshop participants

[6] www.mentimeter.com

additionally have the role of potential users of the ideas, this definition of "expert" was used for the intermediate mutual feedback. The implementation of this kind of mutual assessment in the laboratory experiment in Study III shows that it is not possible to exclude the risk of irrational behavior resulting from it. This probability of biases, e.g., due to group dynamics, was deliberately included again in the present field quasi-experiments, as this score did not have to be representative. It served as the treatment and thus as a possible stimulus for intersubjectivity and was collected separately from the external assessment that determined the performance groups.

6.2.1.1.4 External Assessment (Stage 6)

The completed sketch boards from the two workshop groups were publicly shown in Stage 6 for another posttest at the open innovation lab JOSEPHS in Nuremberg. Altogether, 100 random visitors (50 per workshop group) served as assessors for the external score in Stage 6. In the context of open innovation, these are probably the best experts to be potential users of the ideas (Chesbrough, 2003; Haller et al., 2017). The random visitors voted on the external assessment using the question "*Is the idea understandable?*" again on a rating scale of 0–10 via the online voting tool Mentimeter. To clarify the difference between understandability and the quality of the idea presented, the random visitors were additionally asked to rate their favorite idea.

6.2.1.2 Participants

The experimental design of this study aims to reflect common innovation co-creation settings such as workshops in creative spaces. Both workshop groups had around 10 participants (11 and 9), which is a typical number of participants in a range between 5 and 10 people in such a setting. The groups had different participant compositions and different collaboration modes. The first group with 11 self-selected participants was a homogeneous group in the context of LZE cooperation partners. All were from an engineering environment. The workshop group was already collaborating in an innovation co-creation workshop series for business development. The present field quasi-experiment took place in one of these serial meetings. The task was to find a consumer application for a new portable X-ray device that had been developed by seven members of the group. These are indicated as experts in the technology as shown in Table 6.2.

Table 6.2 Composition of the homogeneous workshop group

COMPOSITION HOMOGENEOUS WORKSHOP GROUP			
Idea no.	Sex	Age	Technology expert
1	m	41	x
2	m	46	
3	m	41	
4	m	46	x
5	m	35–45	x
6	m	39	x
7	m	32	x
8	m	26	
9	m	44	x
10	m	28	x
11	m	43	
Average:	**100%**	**26–46**	**77%**

The second, diverse group with nine participants was explicitly composed for the experiment during an ongoing business development project. The task was to find a consumer application for a new display technology. The goal was to find possible co-creator selection criteria that can be associated with a high degree of intersubjectivity by diversifying the composition of the group. Therefore, the workshop group was carefully selected to achieve diversity, as male participants are more likely to overestimate themselves (Ehrlinger & Dunning, 2003) and homogenous groups tend to develop distorting group dynamics (Schuurman et al., 2015). Participants were invited using purposive sampling (Bryman & Bell, 2011) to cover a broad range of perspectives and balance possible proximity to the topic.

A distribution of male and female participants, as well as different age groups, was taken into account. Suggestions for co-creator characteristics after Schuurman et al. (2015), such as different professional backgrounds (closeness to consumer market, innovativeness, scholar/practitioner) were likewise considered, as were different levels of technological knowledge and experience with the device to be co-created. The age of the nine workshop participants ranged from 25 to 58, and five identified as male and four as female. Four of them already were familiar with the device. Table 6.3 gives an overview of the group composition.

Table 6.3 Composition of the diverse workshop group

COMPOSITION DIVERSE WORKSHOP GROUP				
IDEA	BACKGROUND	SEX	AGE	FAMILIAR WITH DEVICE
A	business development	m	27	x
B	innovation consulting	f	41	
C	design	f	58	
D	ergonomics consulting	m	50	
E	education management	f	41	
F	academic research	m	26	
G	engineering	m	53	x
H	engineering	m	32	x
I	market intelligence	f	25	x
Average:		**5 m/4f**	**25–58**	**44%**

Together, the two groups had 20 participants to enable comparability with the feedback group in the laboratory experiment. To avoid group dynamics, unequal treatment, or other validity threats, both field quasi-experiments were conducted online via video conference for maximum replicability and controllability.

6.2.2 Hypotheses

Study III found that feedback on understandability of the creation may reduce overestimation and stimulate co-creators to move their self-assessment towards feedback. Despite all these movements, the average self-assessment actually remained the same. Intersubjectivity, understood as an aligning of self-assessments with feedback, did not increase. This is what the present field quasi-experiment seeks to confirm with Hypothesis 1.

Hypothesis 1: *"The mean self-assessment of participants will not change after feedback."*

It was previously found that there are no learning effects in the short term. It would therefore be interesting to know whether participants with intersubjective traits can be identified early through a mutual feedback stage. In contrast to the laboratory experiment, this is possible in the present study because the external assessment provided a comparative measure. Assuming from the laboratory experiment that mutual feedback could be analogous to external feedback, the

Dunning-Kruger test is used to determine the later performance groups for the external assessment from the mutual feedback. Ideas that are individually overestimated may be discarded in this way, making it possible to focus on potentially more market-relevant contributions from the third and top quartile. This would eliminate the need to retest co-created ideas, making the process much more efficient. Hypothesis 2 assumes that the mutual assessment feedback and the external assessment show the same tendencies in the Dunning-Kruger test:

Hypothesis 2: *"The mutual assessment feedback reveals the same performance grouping as the external assessment."*

6.2.3 Data Collection and Analysis

All data from this study were collected on a data sheet. Besides measuring static data by subjective feedback, the suggestions of Ehkirch and Matsumae (2024) were followed for measuring dynamic data by determining the movement of self-estimation before and after feedback. In addition, after feedback, participants' reaction behavior was observed, such as a change in their design, possibly in combination with a change in self-assessment, to extend the approach of the laboratory experiment. For the full data sheet, please see Appendix L in the Electronic Supplementary Material.

The data sheet includes

- **Data from the sketch boards:** General characteristics of the participants (age, gender, technology expert/familiar with device) and information about whether they changed their design after feedback
- **Data from the online voting tool:** Self-assessments before (SA_1) and after (SA_2) the feedback, the average mutual feedback (AMA), and the average external assessment (AEA)

The data analysis started with the determination of the mean values. Then, following the results of the previous study, the intersubjective levels before (P_1) and after (P_2) feedback were calculated with the equation $P_t = SA_t - AMA_{t.}$ as the distance between the self-assessment (SA) and the average mutual assessments (AMA). These two values were used to identify the movements in the self-assessment after the feedback. These values additionally enable the determination of overestimators and underestimators. Following the last study, a self-assessment was again defined as a "sufficiently precise" estimate if it was located within the radius of one point from the average mutual assessments. A detailed example of the "sufficiently precise" estimate is presented in Fig. 5.2 in Study III.

The last step of the data analysis involved assigning the participants to the four performance groups after the Dunning-Kruger test. These were calculated by determining the quartiles of the average external assessments (AEA) of each sketch board. All participants whose AEA value fell below a quartile boundary were assigned to the respective performance group. An overview of the quartile boundaries of both workshop groups is given in Table 6.4.

Table 6.4 Quartile boundaries of workshop groups after Schlösser et al. (2013)

QUARTILE BOUNDARIES DUNNING-KRUGER TEST			
HOMOGENEOUS GROUP		DIVERSE GROUP	
External assessment	Quartile	External assessment	Quartile
5.1	1	4.9	1
5.8	2	6.1	2
6.2	3	7.7	3
6.9	4	8.2	4

The full Dunning-Kruger test was then obtained by comparing the quartiles of the self-assessments before (SA_1) and after (SA_2) the feedback and the average mutual assessment. If the test takes a standard course, participants are typically divided into overestimators (bottom and second quartile), correct estimators (third quartile), and underestimators (top quartile).

6.3 Field Quasi-Experiment I: Homogeneous Workshop group

The workshop group in Field Quasi-Experiment I had a homogeneous composition of male participants from an engineering environment and a high level of expertise in their technological field. The group had been formed through self-selection in the context of LZE cooperation partners. At the time of the field quasi-experiment, the group had already conducted several similar innovation and co-creation workshops on the same topic. This workshop group represented an actual, established practice of innovation co-creation.

6.3.1 Experimental Protocol: Homogeneous Workshop Group

The first field quasi-experiment in Study IV lasted 90 minutes and took place as part of a series of co-creation workshops with an already established homogeneous workshop group from an engineering business environment. The age of the 11 male workshop participants ranged from 26 to 46. The task was to find a consumer application for a new portable X-ray device that had been developed by seven members of the group. These are indicated as experts in the technology.

After a brief introduction to the procedure and a verification that all participants were able to use the sketch boards correctly, the participants started with Stage 1. All questions during the workshop were answered by the conducting researcher via chat or during break-out sessions.

6.3.2 Findings: Homogeneous Workshop Group

All scores in Experiment I were above 4 out of 10 points and demonstrate a generally high-quality perception of the developed ideas. This high valuation meant that comparatively few participants were in the range of "sufficiently precise" self-assessments, demonstrated in Fig. 6.2.

With four correct estimators before and after the feedback, the proportion of "sufficiently precise" self-assessments stays at 36%. These still corrected their self-assessments, and two participants changed types after the feedback.

The overestimation by the participants could not be denied: Before the feedback, 8 out of 11 overestimated themselves. Surprisingly, after the feedback (which consequently turned out negatively for the majority of workshop participants), only one of them still underestimated himself and 10 overestimated themselves. Seven clearly overestimated themselves several times and appeared to be untroubled by the mutual feedback. There were no correct estimators.

The movement of self-estimation after feedback was not clearly distinct in any direction, neither towards the feedback nor away from it. Only about one third of participants (36.5%) tried to correct their self-assessment at all, as shown in Fig. 6.3. Another third (36.5%) did not change their (wrong) self-assessment at all, and the remaining 27% were undiscerning and even moved their self-assessments away from the score of the mutual assessment feedback. This means that more than two-thirds of the participants were resistant to feedback on the understandability of their creations.

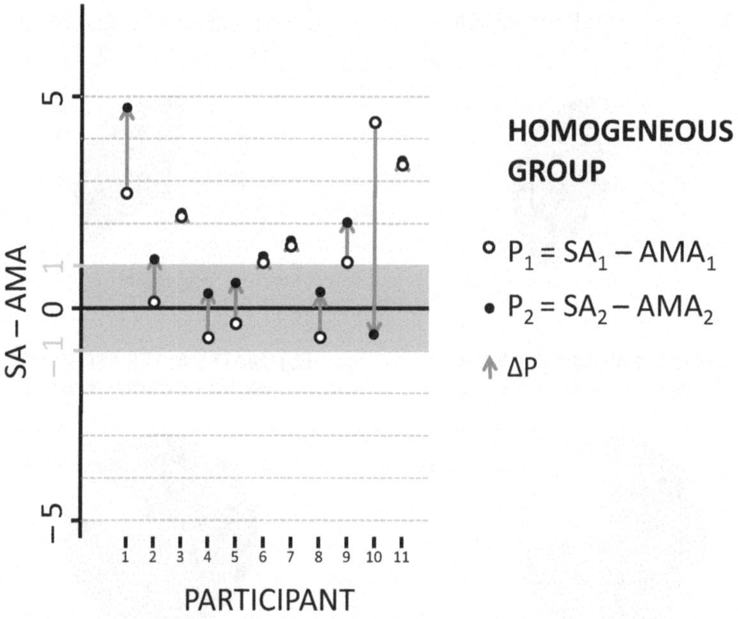

Fig. 6.2 Movement of self-assessment in the homogeneous workshop group

Sequencing the task made it possible to observe the participants' behavior when designing the sketch boards and to measure the change in self-assessment—for example, whether participants changed their design after the feedback stage. The behavior there was similar to the self-assessment: While a majority (82%) of the workshop participants changed their design and/or their self-assessment after the mutual assessment feedback, they did not necessarily do this towards the feedback. Moreover, a surprising number of the participants (18%) did not react at all to the mutual assessment feedback. Here, too, a kind of feedback resistance is evident.

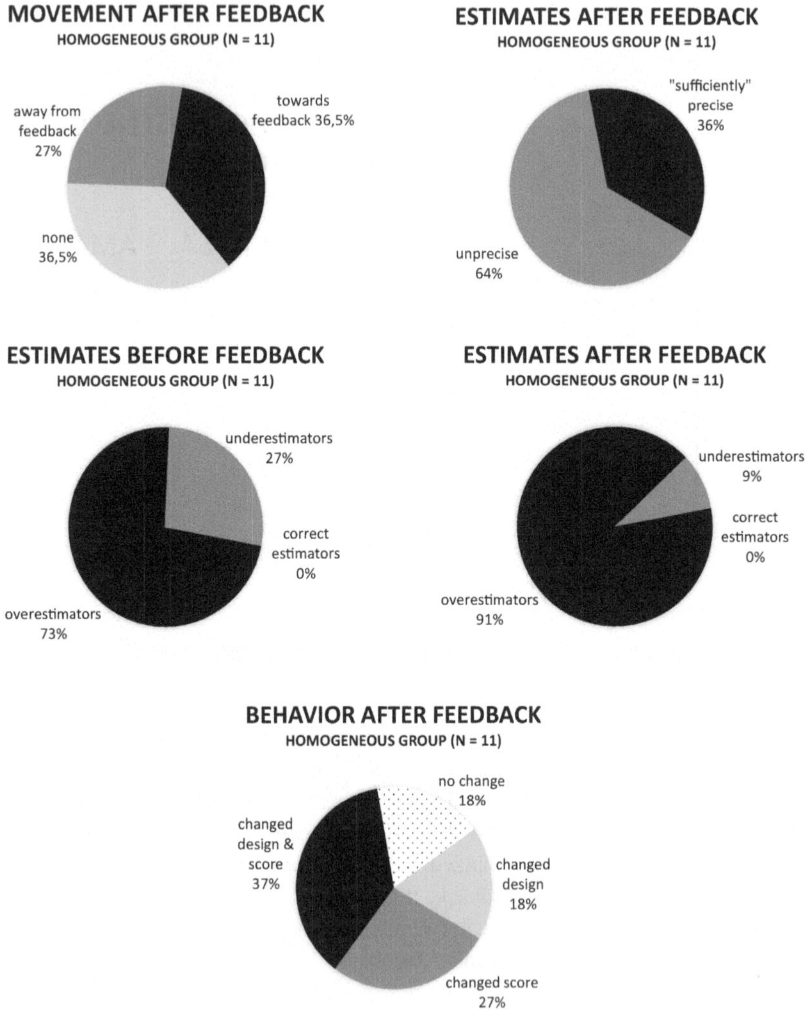

Fig. 6.3 Behavior with feedback in the homogeneous workshop group

6.3.2.1 Hypothesis 1: Change of Mean Self-Assessment

Since the feedback was negative for the majority of participants, one would expect that the mean self-assessment would decrease after the feedback, or at least remain the same, as was observed in the laboratory experiment. Yet Hypothesis 1 must be rejected for the homogeneous workshop group because the opposite unexpectedly occurred: Overall, the mean self-assessment before feedback was 8.3 points—and it rose to 8.5 points after feedback, as presented in Fig. 6.4. Accordingly, the mean overestimation of 2.5 increased slightly after the mutual feedback to 2.7. Additionally, the mean mutual assessment feedback with 6.9 points was clearly above the mean actual score of 5.8 given by the external assessments in the innovation lab.

6.3.2.2 Hypothesis 2: Identification of Performance Groups

A comparison with the Dunning-Kruger effect shows the extent of overestimation in this field quasi-experiment in Fig. 6.5. A typical Dunning-Kruger pattern with crossing scores in the third quartile does not occur. The self-assessment is higher by a mean of 2.5, although there is still a visible downward trend in self-assessment in the third quartile before feedback, which indicates a more realistic self-assessment in the top quartile. After feedback, however, just these top performers corrected their self-assessment upward.

The progression of mutual assessment feedback shows a similar tendency to the external assessment, at a higher level. The mutual assessment feedback reveals the same performance grouping as the external assessment in all four quartiles. This clearly confirms Hypothesis 2. In this experiment, it would have been possible to identify the participants in the third and top quartile as early as the mutual feedback stage. The most promising ideas from participants with the highest intersubjectivity levels could have been identified after the first task. In the present experiment, the two top performer groups would still have considerably overestimated themselves.

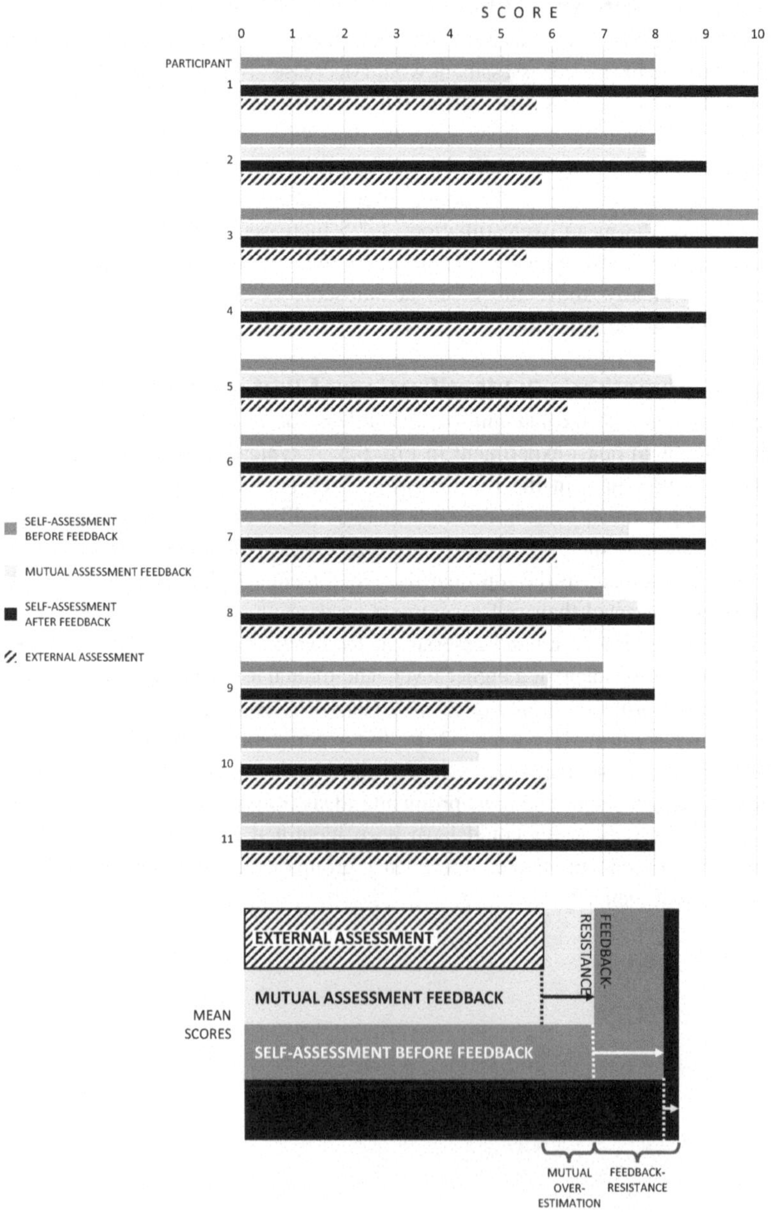

Fig. 6.4 Individual results and mean scores in the homogeneous workshop group

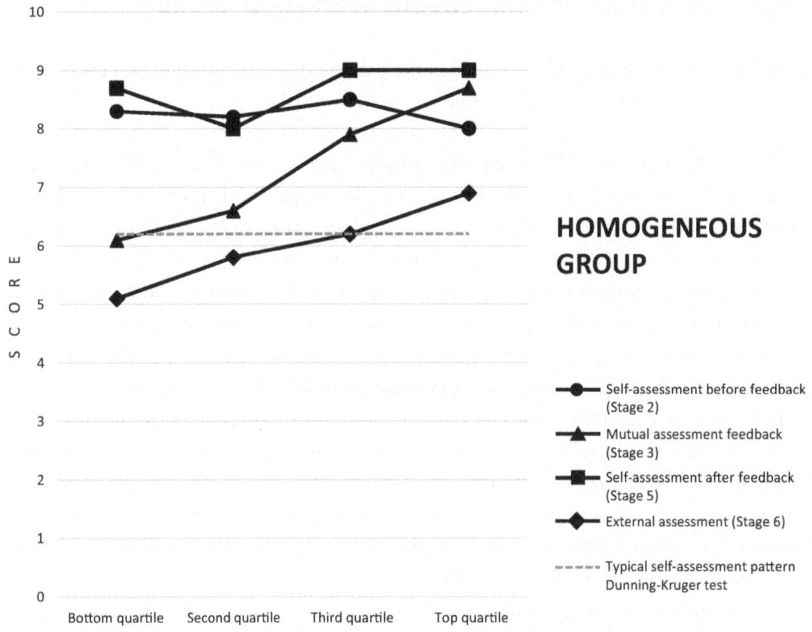

Fig. 6.5 Results of the Dunning-Kruger test: Homogeneous workshop group

The results suggest that it is harder than expected to influence co-creators to share their understanding with other users: The workshop participants exhibit an overestimation that even exceeds the investigated Dunning-Kruger test. The data reveal a much higher mean overestimation, by 2.5 points before feedback on a scale of 0–10. The renewed increase of overestimation by 0.2 points after predominantly negative feedback is a clear sign of a lack of learning effect in terms of intersubjectivity. This is supported by the result that nearly two-thirds of the workshop participants were not aligning with feedback. Most of the co-creators in this homogeneous workshop seem incapable of learning through feedback and of increasing their intersubjectivity over time. After predominantly negative feedback, many of them shift their self-assessment even higher, away from the feedback.

6.3.3 Discussion: Homogeneous Workshop Group

Field Quasi-Experiment I demonstrates how the realistic evaluation of co-creation ideas is surpassed by mutual estimation, and is further surpassed by individual estimation, which even increases after negative feedback. Even though this was a particularly realistic field quasi-experiment with a co-creator group that was already collaborating in a workshop series, the overall high level of overestimation is not surprising. This is due to the composition of the workshop group and their professional proximity to the project: Male participants are more likely to overestimate themselves (Dunning, 2011; Ehrlinger & Dunning, 2003). Moreover, such homogenous co-creator groups tend towards detrimental group dynamics like niche thinking and one-dimensional contributions. The most realistic results can be achieved with diversity in workshop groups (Schuurman et al., 2015).

Diversity is essential—both personally and professionally. For the majority of the workshop participants, the test was about a self-developed technology, which might have caused a double over-estimation due to own work results in combination with own application ideas (Kahnemann et al., 1990). The workshop participants' engineering expertise could have similarly led to distortions like over-requirement (Shmueli et al., 2012).

The impact of feedback was surprising. In contrast to an expected stability in the face of feedback (Kruger & Dunning, 1999; Pallier et al., 2002; Schlösser et al., 2013) or a learning effect resulting in less overestimation (Krajc & Ortmann, 2008; Mayo et al., 2012; Murphy, 2017), there was actually an increase in overestimation. When exposed to feedback, co-creators apparently take a defensive attitude regarding their own ideas. This feedback-resistance effect sheds new light on the behavior of individuals in open innovation.

6.4 Field Quasi-Experiment II: Diverse Workshop Group

The workshop group in Field Quasi-Experiment II had a diverse composition with co-creators selected specifically for an innovation co-creation workshop. The selection was based on a variety of criteria, such as male and female participants, a wide range of ages, and different professional backgrounds such as consumer market proximity, innovativeness, and scholar/practitioner. Only about half of the participants were familiar with the new display technology involved in the task. This diverse group was purposely composed as differently as possible from the previous homogeneous group in order to draw conclusions about co-creator selection criteria and their implementation.

6.4.1 Experimental Protocol: Diverse Workshop Group

The second field quasi-experiment in Study IV lasted 75 minutes and took place with a diverse workshop group, which was specifically composed for the experiment. The task was to find a consumer application for a new display technology. The age of the nine workshop participants ranged from 25 to 58, five identified as male and four as female. Four of them were already familiar with the device.

Since the workshop group was newly composed and some of the participants were not familiar with the display technology in the task, an expert from the project team at LZE gave a brief introduction to the device and its features. The workshop then applied the identical setup and procedure: The participants started with Stage 1 after a brief introduction to the procedure and a verification that all participants were able to use the sketch boards correctly. As questions arose during the workshop, they were answered by the conducting researcher via chat or during breakout sessions.

6.4.2 Findings: Diverse Workshop Group

The scores of the diverse workshop were all on a high level over 4 points out of 10, as shown in Fig. 6.6. Thus, the overall results of the second group were as diverse as its composition. There was a high level of imprecise self-assessments. Two out of the nine participants were in the range of “sufficiently precise” self-assessments in comparison to the mutual assessment feedback. Only one of them stayed in the precise range after the feedback.

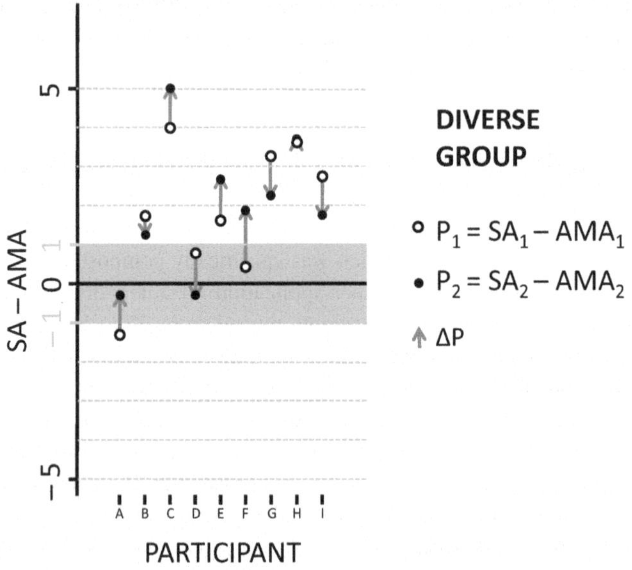

Fig. 6.6 Movement of self-assessment in the diverse workshop group

The diverse workshop group participants overestimated themselves significantly: Before the feedback, six out of nine overestimated themselves. Mutual assessment feedback was negative for the majority of seven participants, with a mean score of 5.8, well below the external assessment of 6.4. The same six overestimating participants still overestimated themselves the second time, despite feedback. No correct estimators could be determined here either.

In terms of behavior after feedback, all workshop participants changed their design and/or their self-assessment after the mutual assessment feedback this time, although again not necessarily towards the feedback, as shown in Fig. 6.7. Just over half of the participants (56%) moved their self-estimations towards the feedback. Nevertheless, just under half showed irrational behavior by either not changing their self-estimation despite feedback (33%) or even being undiscerning by changing it in the opposite direction, away from the score of the mutual feedback (11%).

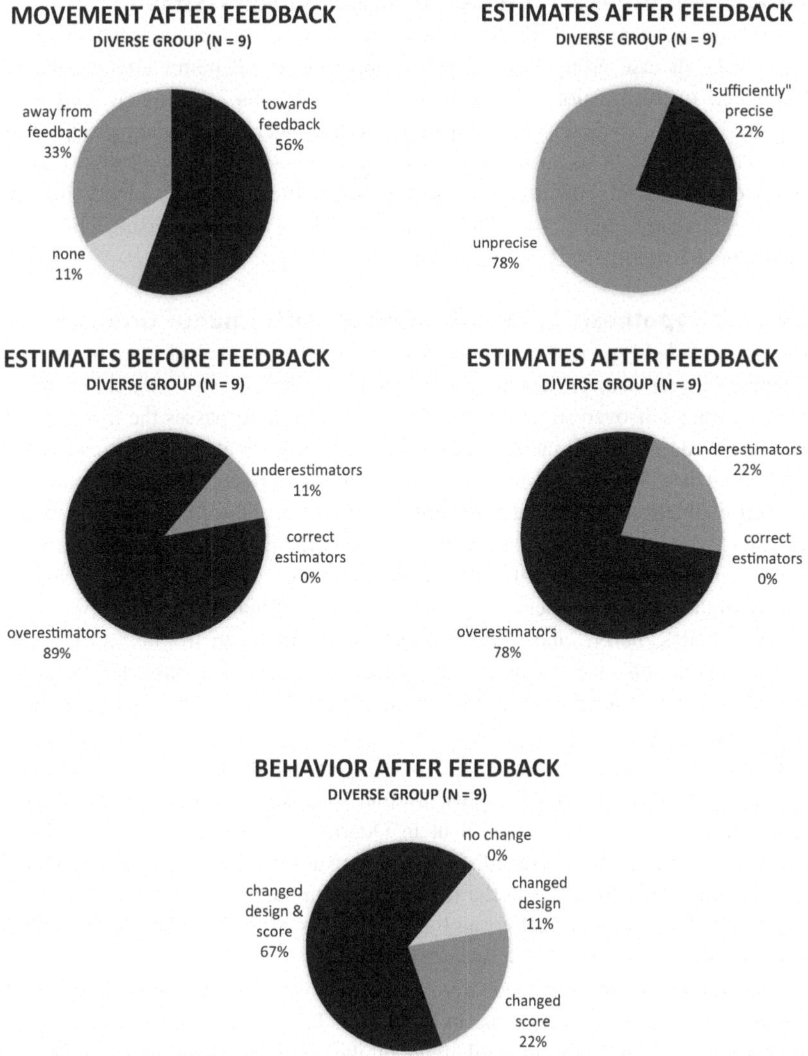

Fig. 6.7 Behavior with feedback in the diverse workshop group

6.4.2.1 Hypothesis 1: Change of Mean Self-Assessment

Fig. 6.8 on the next page illustrates how the mean self-assessment before feedback in the diverse group was 7.7 points and rose to 7.8 points after feedback. The mean overestimation of 1.3 increased to 1.4 after the mutual feedback. Hypothesis 1 must therefore be rejected for the diverse workshop group. The 0.1 point increase in mean overestimation, with two-thirds of workshop participants overestimating themselves a second time after receiving predominantly negative feedback, indicates a lack of learning in terms of intersubjectivity in Field Quasi-Experiment II.

6.4.2.2 Hypothesis 2: Identification of Performance Groups

The second field quasi-experiment shows an almost typical pattern of the Dunning-Kruger test, presented in Fig. 6.9. Nevertheless, an overarching, more or less strong self-overestimation could be observed. It surpasses the investigated Dunning-Kruger test and increased to feedback-resistance after the mutual assessment feedback. The typical pattern of the Dunning-Kruger test is illustrated by the self-estimations regarding intersubjectivity in the bottom, third, and fourth quartiles, which are approximately identical, and their resulting overlap with the actual score in Quartile 3. Only participants in Quartile 2 rated themselves significantly higher than the others. Yet there is an overestimation of intersubjectivity in all quartiles, before and after feedback. Participants in the bottom quartile corrected their self-assessment downward by a mean of 0.4 points after receiving mutual assessment feedback and missed the pattern line at 7.2 by only 0.1 points, self-assessing at 7.3.

Compared to their external assessment, participants typically overestimate themselves by a mean of 2.9 points. Mutual assessment feedback most closely approximates the external assessment in Quartile 2, and with this the realistic value of the ideas there. Nevertheless, participants in Quartile 2 assess themselves significantly higher than the remaining group and miss their mean external assessment by 2.2 points before and even 3 points after feedback. Here, a kind of resistance to feedback becomes most apparent.

The mutual assessment feedback is considerably different from the external assessment as both measures cross in Quartile 2. That said, the mutual assessment feedback still follows the upward trend of the external assessment and identifies the same performance groups in quartiles 1, 2, and 4 correctly, supporting Hypothesis 2. For Quartile 3, the hypothesis must be rejected. This performance group unexpectedly received the worst mutual assessment feedback of the entire group.

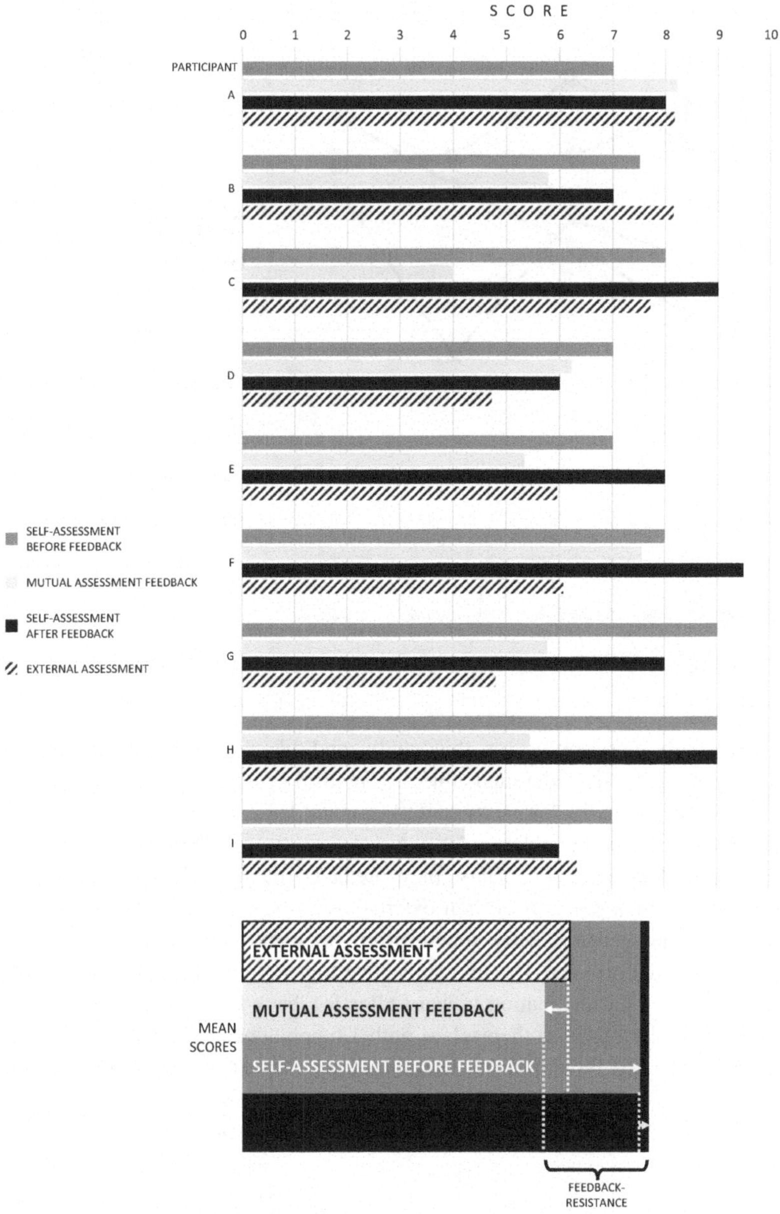

Fig. 6.8 Individual results and mean scores in the diverse group

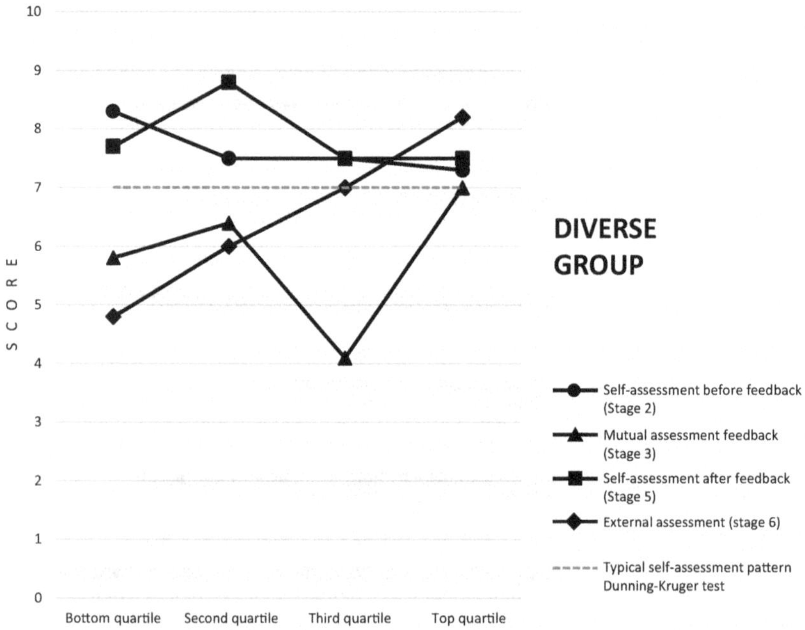

Fig. 6.9 Results of the Dunning-Kruger test in the diverse workshop group

Particularly noteworthy for this study, and likewise characteristic of the Dunning-Kruger test, is the intersubjective realism of the participants in Quartile 3. Despite receiving the lowest mutual assessment feedback of the entire group—4.1, which is 3.1 points below their external assessment—they remained firm in their self-evaluation at 7.5. Thus, they predicted their "real" result quite precisely with just 0.3 points over their external assessment. These participants were undeterred and seemed clearly convinced of the market-relevance of their ideas beyond individual biases. The intersubjective top performers in Quartile 4 similarly corrected their estimation upward after feedback by a mean of 0.2 points. Since they underestimated themselves with 1.6 points before and 1.4 points after feedback, which is typical of the Dunning-Kruger test, they have hit the mutual assessment feedback quite precisely with 0.3 points before and 0.5 points after feedback. This demonstrates their high degree of intersubjectivity.

6.4.3 Discussion: Diverse Workshop Group

The diverse workshop group shows a slight increase of mean overestimation regarding intersubjectivity after feedback. The feedback resistance effect, however, is not very evident in this workshop group. Although many participants were significantly off in their self-assessments, some were able to predict their external assessments almost accurately, demonstrating high intersubjectivity, especially in Quartile 3. A look at the background of this quartile is therefore worthwhile: The two participants were the youngest (25) and oldest (58) across both groups, so age seems not to matter. They have a design and market intelligence background—professions that inherently require a high level of intersubjectivity. This correspondingly applies to the two top performers in the top quartile, who have professional backgrounds where a high degree of realistic user knowledge can be expected: business developer and innovation consultant. What these four top performers have in common is the closeness of their professions to the market. Focusing on this characteristic when selecting co-creators may considerably increase the efficiency of open innovation through intersubjectivity.

Beyond that, three of these four participants in quartiles 3 and 4 were female, which may affect self-estimation, as male participants are more likely to overestimate themselves and find it harder to adapt to feedback (Dunning, 2011; Ehrlinger & Dunning, 2003; Mayo, 2016). This effect is particularly evident in Quartile 2 which contains only male participants and shows the highest overestimation and feedback resistance of the whole group. Their research and engineering backgrounds, which are more distant from the consumer market than other professions in the group, may have contributed to the misjudgment in this case. The technical expertise of the participants who were already familiar with the device could additionally account for the overestimation (Shmueli et al., 2012). This is countered by the fact that one participant in each of the top two quartiles 3 and 4 already knew the device and demonstrated more intersubjectivity. The participants' professional background is probably more decisive than their knowledge of the respective technology. It is similarly reflected in the theory that co-creators with high technical skills are more likely to produce technically feasible ideas, while trend-aware and innovative users produce more novel ideas (Schweitzer et al., 2014).

6.5 Overall Findings: Homogeneous and Diverse Workshop Groups

Looking at the homogeneous and diverse workshop groups together, there are considerably more overestimators in the homogeneous workshop group who are not supported by the external assessment. The higher overestimation in the homogeneous group came with lower intersubjectivity towards the external assessment than the diverse group. The diverse group achieved in Quartile 3 the most realistic user knowledge despite receiving the worst feedback. In Quartile 2, the diverse group showed the strongest movement away from feedback in both experiments. In this group, however, some participants likewise ignored the feedback. This was because they were able to predict their external assessments quite accurately and were therefore right to disregard the mutual feedback.

A comparison of the mean scores of both groups shows a 0.2-point increase in self-assessment after significantly lower feedback in the homogeneous group, while the increase in the diverse group is slightly lower at 0.1 point. The homogeneous group demonstrated higher group intersubjectivity, probably through the existing collaboration, by a mutual overestimation in the feedback stage of 1.1 points. The purposefully assembled diverse group, by contrast, mutually underestimated itself with 0.5 points in the feedback stage. Accordingly, the feedback-resistance behavior was higher in the homogeneous group (63.5%) than in the diverse group (44%).

6.6 Discussion

Study IV demonstrates that co-creators are individuals and behave as such. According to the data, providing feedback to co-creators does not lead to more intersubjectivity overall. The feedback-resistance effect exemplifies how feedback can affect evaluation biases in a previously unknown way. Intersubjectivity may therefore be considered as a new co-creator selection criterion that is easy to determine through a mutual feedback step. Co-creators with an intersubjective trait may be identified through a mutual feedback step about the understandability of their creation. As derived from the data, this works in the majority of cases, even in small groups with nonrandomized, selected participants. Feedback plays an important role in identification, despite a possible feedback-resistance effect. Learning intersubjectivity may not be needed after all: The study found that there are co-creators with realistic user knowledge who do not respond to feedback because they are well able to assess their external assessment and thus the market potential of their ideas. These co-creators are actually the ones who are interesting for selection in innovation co-creation.

The early identification of intersubjective co-creators could be a first step to helping innovating organizations co-create more efficiently. They could assess the market potential and self-assessment traits of co-creators in advance, when asking potential co-creators about the understandability of their work, and thus encourage them to consider the perspectives of other users. This approach could counteract evaluation biases that inhibit the remarkable potential of creative users.

6.6.1 From a Research Perspective

There is a feedback-resistance effect

This study's finding that intersubjectivity is unlearnable under certain conditions contributes to the theoretical discourse on whether it is an inherently personal trait (Krajc & Ortmann, 2008; Kruger & Dunning, 1999; Mayo et al., 2012; Murphy, 2017; Schlösser et al., 2013). Moreover, both experiments in Study IV show a surprising impact of feedback in co-creation workshops. In contrast to expected stability (Kruger & Dunning, 1999; Schlösser et al., 2013), there was actually a slight increase in mean self-assessment. Both field quasi-experiments showed no overall signs of meaningful learning through feedback. When exposed to feedback, some co-creators apparently take a defensive posture with their own ideas. The feedback-resistance effect that was identified sheds new light on the behavior of individuals in open innovation. Unexpected feedback results can be an uncomfortable experience at first. Transforming this into self-awareness and ultimately learning takes time that is not available in most co-creation workshops. Depending on the level of discomfort, self-awareness may not even occur at all (Mayo et al., 2012; Mezirow, 1991).

Intersubjectivity may be a new co-creator selection criterion

Previous research has intensively discussed suitable skills and stages for co-creating (P. Berthon et al., 2011; Hoffman et al., 2010; Kristensson et al., 2004; Oßwald et al., 2019; T. Schweisfurth, 2016; T. G. Schweisfurth & Herstatt, 2015; Schweitzer et al., 2014; von Hippel, 1986). Considering intersubjectivity as an essential co-creation trait beyond expertise like market or technical knowledge might add a new overarching dimension to the selection of co-creators. As this study demonstrates, intersubjectivity is comparatively less difficult to determine during a workshop than other currently discussed skills like innovativeness or creativity (Hoffman et al., 2010) and may be a new overarching selection criterion. Intersubjectivity could complement the user-knowledge skills of co-creator types such as lead users (Huang et al., 2018; Shih et al., 2010; von Hippel, 1986) or emergent nature co-creators (Hoffman et al., 2010; Vernette & Kidar, 2013). In particular, the characteristics of rational thinking and reflection attributed to the emergent nature co-creator type could be well complemented by the trait of intersubjectivity.

6.6.2 From a Managerial Perspective

Mutual feedback can often identify co-creators who have an intersubjective trait

The results imply that feedback does not directly make the co-creation process more efficient. Innovating organizations cannot rely on individual learning effects in terms of intersubjectivity. The study analysis shows that intermediate feedback about the understandability of the co-created ideas could nevertheless provide important information about which co-creators are probably in the top two—especially the third—performance groups in terms of intersubjectivity. They likely create more realistic, market-relevant ideas beyond individual biases. Focusing on these may increase the efficiency of open innovation considerably.

Diversity in workshop groups and co-creators working in professions close to the market both foster intersubjectivity

Generating market-relevance in open innovation is challenging, as co-creators are individually biased (Ariely, 2008). Reaching beyond organizational boundaries with open innovation correspondingly means going beyond an individual estimation. Intersubjectivity is a key skill for taking this step beyond individuality. The present study demonstrates that it might be essential to select co-creators in open innovation workshops in terms of their intersubjective trait. As derived from the data, this could be found in co-creators with backgrounds close to the market. Innovating organizations could reach out for intersubjective co-creators in diverse teams. Study IV additionally introduces how these people could be easily identified through mutual feedback within a workshop. This may present the opportunity to discard individually overestimated ideas at an early stage and focus on potentially more market-relevant contributions. The present research may therefore serve as a basis for composing future co-creation workshops.

Intersubjectivity provides a powerful opportunity for realistic evaluation that can be easily determined

The study analysis aligns with the theory (Krajc & Ortmann, 2008; Kruger & Dunning, 1999; Mayo et al., 2012; Schlösser et al., 2013) that intersubjectivity is a hard-to-learn key trait for efficiency in open innovation. Uninfluential co-creators, who mostly design for themselves, leave companies dependent on individuals with an existing ability for realistic self-estimation. Practitioners might rethink suitable skills for open innovation. The findings of the present study can help innovating organizations that are unsure about selecting co-creators or their ideas—particularly because a selection by the innovating organization can similarly be biased (R. Katz & Allen, 1982). Intersubjectivity provides a powerful opportunity for realistic evaluation that can be easily determined through a mutual feedback stage, as demonstrated in this study.

6.6.3 Summary of Findings

The present study's findings on the impact of feedback to co-creators about the understandability of their creation were two-fold: On the one hand, feedback does not lead to overall intersubjectivity. Feedback to co-creators merely implies an increase in self-estimation and with this a feedback-resistance effect in self-assessment and behavior. This phenomenon is not described in the literature yet and contributes first evidence of a new evaluation bias. On the other hand, mutual feedback in innovation co-creation workshops can, in most cases, help identify co-creators with an intersubjective trait. To foster intersubjectivity in innovation co-creation workshops even more, organizers could select co-creators according to group diversity and to them having professions close to the market. Overall, intersubjectivity could be a new overarching selection criterion for co-creators or it could adapt to existing concepts such as the emergent nature co-creator.

YOUR ITEMS FROM STUDY IV

- There is a feedback-resistance effect in self-assessment and behavior.
- Mutual feedback can often identify co-creators with an intersubjective trait.
- Diversity in workshop groups and co-creators having professions close to the market both foster intersubjectivity.
- Intersubjectivity may be a new co-creator selection criterion.

Summary of Findings and Implications 7

M. Oßwald, *When Co-Creation Leads to Love*, Markt- und Unternehmensentwicklung Markets and Organisations,
https://doi.org/10.1007/978-3-658-48890-1_7

The IKEA effect works best with successful completion of a task and the sharing of the outcomes. Accordingly, this final part concludes the thesis by providing a summary of the findings in Chap. 1. The corresponding implications for open innovation research and for management are described in Chap. 2. This is followed by an outlook from which future research directions can be derived, and by a final conclusion.

7.1 Summary of Findings

Co-creating market relevance for more than one individual user is found to be challenging, as co-creators tend to be individually biased about the value of their contribution. One of the best known of these evaluation biases, the IKEA effect (Norton et al., 2012), provided the basis for this thesis. The work aimed to create a comprehensive and in-depth understanding of evaluation biases and the concept of intersubjectivity as a common understanding of value in innovation co-creation. With an exploratory sequential design, the topic was first approached by qualitative studies I and II for a holistic understanding. The second part with studies III and IV aimed to identify and test new variables on intersubjectivity in several quantitative experiments in the laboratory and in the field. Every chapter provided key findings, which are summarized in Table 7.1.

Study I aimed to systematize evaluation biases. The systematization was based on the IKEA effect (Norton et al., 2012), which triggered the discovery of a plethora of other similar biases. The narrative literature review in Study I identified 29 phenomena related to the IKEA effect, which were systematized in nine overarching topics. These overarching topics provide clarity and guidance in a complex research field and go beyond the previously known reasons for these biases, such as over-commitment (Staw, 1981) and endowment effects (Kahnemann et al., 1990). The topics are *biased ownership, feelings of effectance, invested effort, sustainability, incorporation into the self, control, value transfer, egocentrism,* and *negative impact.*

Table 7.1 Overview of findings

OVERVIEW OF FINDINGS		
RQ: How does intersubjectivity work in open innovation?		
	**Study I: SYSTEMATIZING KNOWN EVALUATION BIASES**	**RQ I: How can evaluation biases be systematized?** • There are nine overarching topics of evaluation biases: biased ownership, feelings of effectance, invested effort, sustainability, incorporation into the self, control, value transfer, egocentrism, and negative impact. • Evaluation biases provide positive and negative impacts on innovation co-creation. • The impact of evaluation biases varies with the empowerment dimensions of the co-creators.
	**Study II: EXPLORING INTERSUBJECTIVITY WITH EXPERTS**	**RQ II: How do evaluation biases impact open innovation practice?** • The need for critical distance changes with roles and stages of the innovation process. • Creating for oneself or for others is the turning point between positive and negative impacts of evaluation biases. • Evaluation biases give co-creators resilience. • Evaluation biases can affect all individual roles as a barrier. • Intersubjectivity could be unlearnable.
	**Study III: EXPERIMENTING WITH INTERSUBJECTIVITY IN THE LABORATORY**	**RQ III: Can co-creators learn intersubjectivity through feedback?** • Intersubjectivity is a trait in itself, unrelated to creativity. • Intersubjectivity can be measured between external (or mutual) assessments and self-assessment. • Understandability is the key dimension for moving self-assessments. • Co-creators react irrationally to feedback.

(continued)

Table 7.1 (continued)

OVERVIEW OF FINDINGS		
RQ: How does intersubjectivity work in open innovation?		
	**Study IV: EXPERIMENTING WITH INTERSUBJECTIVITY IN THE FIELD**	**RQ IV: Can co-creators learn intersubjectivity through feedback about the understandability of their creation?** • There is a feedback-resistance effect in self-assessment and behavior. • Mutual feedback can often identify co-creators with an intersubjective trait. • Diversity in workshop groups and co-creators having professions close to the market both foster intersubjectivity. • Intersubjectivity may be a new co-creator selection criterion.

Study I was closely linked with Study II through an iteration process of the literature selection. The iteration of literature, together with the academic and intermediary experts, revealed additional biases due to egocentrism (Alicke & Govorun, 2005; Kruger & Dunning, 1999; Miller & Ross, 1975; Pallier et al., 2002) with a high probability of negatively impacting the innovation project (Arkes & Blumer, 1985; Biyalogorsky et al., 2006; Boudreau et al., 2012; Katz & Allen, 1982; Schmidt & Calantone, 1998; Thomas & Alluru, 2016). Knowing what biases to watch for when engaging co-creators and where the potential pitfalls lie may be of particular interest to practitioners. Moreover, it was found that the impact of evaluation biases differs with the fields of co-creator empowerment dimensions (Maier & Baccarella, 2024). It was derived that there might be a turning point from positive to negative impact between the dimensions "by me for one" and "by me for many." Two phenomena are the exception in which a transfer of benefits to third-party use is possible: The handmade effect (Fuchs et al., 2015) and the innovation effect of user design (Schreier et al., 2013).

Study II then refined and further explored the findings from the literature review with 12 authors, academic experts, and intermediaries. The goal of the qualitative interview study was to create a holistic overview on how evaluation biases impact open innovation practice. It was discovered that there is a varying need for intersubjectivity, which changes with individual roles and stages of the innovation process, similar to the need for consumer involvement (Atakan et al., 2014). This again raised the question of a turning point between the positive and negative impacts of evaluation biases. This time, the turning point was more clearly defined as "creating for oneself or for others." Evaluation biases may be problematic in all empowerment dimensions other than "by me for one" (Maier & Baccarella, 2024). This is a particularly important finding for innovation co-creation, where the use of the idea by others is intended from the outset.

Moreover, Study II revealed that evaluation biases can induce perseverance in overcoming risks and challenges during the innovation process. Evaluation biases can, however, act as a need or a barrier in all individual roles: co-creators, intermediaries, experts, and even the innovating organization. As a barrier, it can negatively impact risk assessment and the selection of co-created ideas by the organizer or experts. To handle such needs and barriers in co-creator subjectivity, a plethora of methods have been devised for balancing intersubjectivity: creativity methods, involvement design, catalyzation, and external assessment. Finally, the study showed that intersubjectivity might be unlearnable, which would make it a trait that should serve as a selection criterion for co-creators. The learnability of intersubjectivity is highly discussed in the theory (Krajc & Ortmann, 2008; Kruger & Dunning, 1999; Mayo et al., 2012; Murphy, 2017; Pallier et al., 2002; Schlösser et al., 2013). As a result, this element was examined in more detail in Study III.

In order find suitable variables for subsequent field experiments on the learnability of intersubjectivity, Study III explored possible measurements of intersubjectivity at a fixed point in time to extend the recommendations of Ehkirch & Matsumae (2024). The investigation marks the change from qualitative methods to quantitative methods in this thesis. Study III was conducted with a laboratory experiment by examining two groups with 20 participants each. It was shown that assessment movements can be determined as a distance between average external (or mutual) assessments and self-assessment at a fixed point in time. With this approach, intersubjectivity may be better calculated in the future.

Furthermore, it was found that creativity and intersubjectivity do not correlate as may be assumed from co-creator characteristics (P. Berthon et al., 2011; Bogers et al., 2017). Intersubjectivity could be seen as a stand-alone characteristic of co-creators, separate to their creativity. Nonetheless, the integration of several creativity tests (Hocevar, 1980; O'Quin & Besemer, 1989; Williams, 1980) into the experimental design revealed possible dimensions that influence the intersubjectivity of co-creators: The question about the understandability of a creation may be a main driver for the personal development of co-creators' intersubjectivity. It stimulates the most movements in self-assessment and mitigates overestimation by moving it towards the feedback. At the same time, this surprisingly does not lead to more alignment of the self-assessments with the feedback; co-creators continue to behave irrationally after feedback.

The irrational behavior of co-creators after feedback was further explored in two field quasi-experiments with 9 and 11 participants in different workshop group compositions in Study IV. To investigate the question about understandability in greater depth, another external feedback step with 50 participants each was added. This was done to ensure practical suitability of the findings from Study III. Unexpectedly, indications of a possible new phenomenon were found. A feedback-resistance effect in self-assessment and behavior occurred in both groups. The mean self-assessment rose after predominantly negative feedback. Nevertheless, the mutual feedback step on understandability predicted in seven out of eight cases which co-creators are probably in the two top performance groups in terms of intersubjectivity. These groups likely create more realistic, market-relevant ideas beyond individual biases. The findings about intersubjectivity dimensions as well as the unlearnability of intersubjectivity contribute to current theoretical discussions on the topic (Krajc & Ortmann, 2008; Kruger & Dunning, 1999; Mayo et al., 2012; Murphy, 2017; Pallier et al., 2002; Schlösser et al., 2013). Further investigation found characteristics that probably correlate with intersubjectivity. The comparison within and between the groups identified diversity in workshop groups and co-creators having professions close to the market as criteria that foster intersubjectivity.

7.2 Triangulated Findings

The overall research question of this thesis was, "How does intersubjectivity work in open innovation?" The exploratory mixed method approach allows data triangulation from qualitative and quantitative studies with experts, in the laboratory, and in different innovation co-creation workshops (Morse, 1991; Rossman & Wilson, 1985). These different approaches enable a holistic picture of how intersubjectivity works in open innovation (Patton, 2015; Teddlie & Tashakkori, 2009). The findings of this thesis were largely consolidated in the course of the studies, particularly concerning the requiring and the learning of intersubjectivity to answer the overall research question.

7.2.1 Requiring Intersubjectivity

Empirical data from the literature review in Study I and the corresponding expert interviews in Study II show that the requirement for intersubjectivity in open innovation can be derived by asking "when?" (which stages of the innovation process require intersubjectivity?), "who?" (which roles require intersubjectivity?), and "how?" (which empowerment dimensions require intersubjectivity?), as demonstrated in Fig. 7.1.

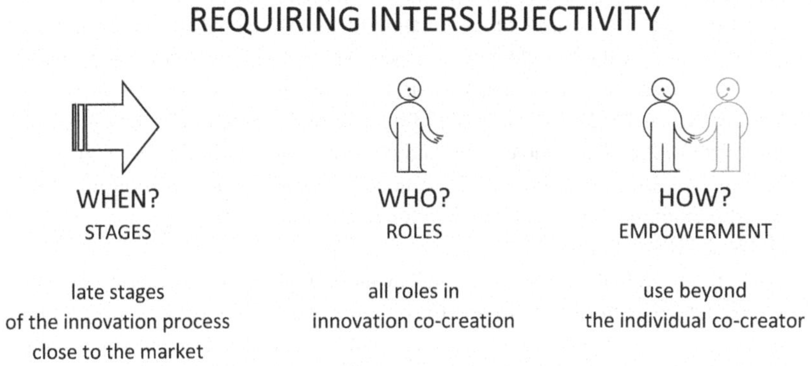

Fig. 7.1 Derived requirement for intersubjectivity in open innovation. (Author's illustration)

The overall findings suggest that intersubjectivity is not universally required in an innovation co-creation process, similar to the varying need for consumer involvement (Atakan et al., 2014). In many cases, evaluation biases do not pose a risk or can support the innovation goal, for example by enhancing the co-creators' resilience and motivation. The critical key issues for requiring intersubjectivity according to the experts were derived from the data as follows:

- WHEN: STAGES
  In early innovation process stages like ideation, the intersubjectivity of the co-creators is not mandatory, since the focus is on the creativity and on collecting individual ideas. Evaluation biases are found to be particularly helpful in these early stages of the innovation process. The closer the stages get to the market, however, the more intersubjectivity is required. Intersubjectivity there provides a realistic assessment for identifying a possible market potential beyond the individual.
- WHO: ROLES
  Since all actors in an innovation co-creation process are additionally potential users, the conscious distinction between individual opinion and the "other" role through intersubjectivity is relevant for every participant in an innovation co-creation process. Yet the ambivalent nature of evaluation biases, which are

beneficial in the early stages and become riskier closer to the market, only applies to co-creators. As derived from the data, intermediaries, innovating organizations, or other external experts for assessment require an extremely high level of intersubjectivity to perform their decision-making roles appropriately. Biases may negatively affect the risk assessment and particularly the selection and assessment of co-created ideas by the organizer or external experts. This issue is reflected in a variety of management-related evaluation biases with negative impact, such as the not-invented-here syndrome ((R. Katz & Allen, 1982) and overcommitment in management (Schmidt & Calantone, 1998). Another related issue is the more critical attitude that comes with higher expertise, as described in the novelty paradox (Boudreau et al., 2012) and the Dunning-Kruger effect (Kruger & Dunning, 1999).

- HOW: EMPOWERMENT
  As long as evaluation biases stay at an individual level, they create benefits. These benefits can turn into risks for efficient innovation processes once other users are involved. The use of ideas beyond the individual co-creator certainly requires intersubjectivity between both individuals. Based on the insights of the empirical part, evaluation biases may be problematic in all empowerment dimensions other than "by me for one" (Maier & Baccarella, 2024). This is a particularly important finding for innovation co-creation, where the use of the idea by others is intended from the outset.

7.2.2 Influencing Self-Assessments

This thesis investigated influencing the self-assessments, and with that the intersubjectivity of co-creators, using a variety of approaches: with qualitative and quantitative methods, with experts from academia and practice, in the laboratory, and in realistic co-creation workshops. Learning effects are a crucial aspect for the impact of intersubjectivity in open innovation. If they cannot be determined, selection and identification possibilities for intersubjective co-creators need to be found to increase the efficiency of innovation co-creation. The qualitative approaches of studies I and II identified contradictory positions on the learnability of intersubjectivity in theory (Krajc & Ortmann, 2008; Kruger & Dunning, 1999; Mayo et al., 2012; Murphy, 2017; Pallier et al., 2002; Schlösser et al., 2013) and in practice. The expert positions ranged from "with the right tools, you can teach it very quickly," to "some can, some have a hard time," to "only a few can." The unlearnability of intersubjectivity was reinforced in the subsequent quantitative approaches of Study III in the laboratory and Study IV in the field.

The impact of feedback was surprising. Feedback is usually found to be a success factor for open innovation projects and contributes to learning in co-creators (Roth et al., 2017). In contrast to the corporate innovation communities studied in that publication, learning through feedback does not seem to apply to the co-creator workshops in the experiments performed for this thesis. In contrast to the expected learning effects producing a decline in overestimation (Krajc & Ortmann, 2008; Mayo et al., 2012; Murphy, 2017), or stability in the face of feedback (Kruger & Dunning, 1999; Pallier et al., 2002; Schlösser et al., 2013), there was actually an average increase of overestimation, going as far as a feedback-resistance effect.

Researchers and practitioners note that the repetition of tasks, combined with financial incentives and feedback, may induce learning effects in self-assessment (Krajc & Ortmann, 2008; Murphy, 2017). The incentivization and task repetition in Study III, however, did not reveal meaningful overall learning effects for intersubjectivity. The investigated question about the understandability of the creation can lead co-creators to change their self-assessment, though in an irrational way. This is particularly true for overestimators, who often move their self-assessment towards the feedback and beyond. Some participants in the experiments in Study IV showed this behavior, too.

In Study IV, another remarkable group of participants emerged. The feedback-resistance effect was discovered in self-assessment and behavior when processing the tasks. The first field quasi-experiment with the homogeneous group revealed a striking share (18%) of co-creators who, after receiving feedback that was significantly different to their self-assessment, did not move at all, neither in their self-assessments, nor in the further processing of their tasks. This lack of effort in some co-creators was similarly described by several experts in Study II. According to the data, self-closing of co-creators is attributed to overly strong evaluation biases or professional experience, which can lead to more efficiency thinking. It could be that some co-creators enjoy the process of co-creating itself and therefore do not care about the results, as recently discovered in the one-away effect (Ruan et al., 2024). It was additionally observed that most top performers in intersubjectivity are not deterred by mutual group feedback, as they are good at assessing the actual market potential of their ideas. This demonstrates that feedback-resistance does not necessarily mean a lack of intersubjectivity.

To conclude, meaningful learning effects regarding intersubjectivity within a workshop could not be observed over the course of several studies and with a variety of approaches. Empirical results suggest that any attempts to influence the self-assessment of co-creators lead to irrational behavior. According to a long-term study by Mayo et al. (2012), it is suspected that up to six months may be required to incorporate feedback into self-awareness and ultimately learning. In an open innovation context, this might be far too much time and effort to invest in co-creator training. Moreover, learning theory notes that unexpected feedback may be accompanied by an unpleasant experience. Depending on the level of discomfort, self-awareness may not even occur at all (Mezirow, 1991). This seems to be the case with the learnability of intersubjectivity through feedback, as intersubjectivity is obviously a trait and not a skill. In addition to the resulting need to select intersubjective co-creators, the experts in Study II suggested several methods that can be used to balance intersubjectivity rather than learning effects. These balancing methods are creativity methods, involvement design, catalyzation, and external assessment.

7.3 Implications

The holistic mixed method exploratory approach of this thesis reveals significant implications for open innovation research and for managing the integration of the concept of intersubjectivity. These implications complement the summary and triangulation of findings highlighted in the previous section. Implications for open innovation research address contributions to the systematization of evaluation biases, intersubjectivity measurements, learning phenomena such as the feedback-resistance effect, and co-creator selection criteria. Implications for management were compiled into a proposal for an intersubjectivity working model to identify, measure, and balance intersubjectivity.

7.3.1 Implications for Open Innovation Research

This thesis contributes various aspects to open innovation research, particularly in the field of innovation co-creation. The empirical part of this thesis yields a number of implications, ranging from the systematization of evaluation biases, the determination of intersubjective levels, the feedback-resistance effect, the learnability of intersubjectivity, to intersubjectivity as a selection criterion for co-creators. These are presented in the following sections.

7.3.1.1 Comprehensive Systematization of Evaluation Biases

The identification and systematization of 29 evaluation biases in this work creates a holistic overview of evaluation biases in open innovation. It provides clarity and guidance in this previously fuzzy research field and contributes to bias literature

(Ariely, 2008) and bias collections (Morrissette, 2021). The nine overarching topics identified go beyond the previously known reasons for these biases, such as overcommitment (Staw, 1981) and endowment effects (Kahnemann et al., 1990), and significantly widen the scope of the research field. The nine topics are *biased ownership, feelings of effectance, invested effort, sustainability, incorporation into the self, control, value transfer, egocentrism,* and *negative impact.* It was additionally identified which biases entail a high probability of negative impact on the innovation project (Arkes & Blumer, 1985; Biyalogorsky et al., 2006; Boudreau et al., 2012; Katz & Allen, 1982; Schmidt & Calantone, 1998; Thomas & Alluru, 2016). Moreover, it could be derived that the turning point between positive and negative impacts of evaluation biases lies between co-creating for oneself and for others. This insight extends previous research on co-creator empowerment dimensions (Maier & Baccarella, 2024).

7.3.1.2 Determination of Intersubjective Levels between Individual Roles

The present work contributes new measurements for intersubjectivity at fixed time points. The advantage of this approach is that the measurement can be done between different individual roles, even beyond co-creator groups, e.g., towards the user. Intersubjectivity (P_t) may be determined as a distance between average mutual (or external) assessments (AMA) and self-assessment (SA) at a fixed measurement point in time t with the equation $P_t = SA_t - AMA_t$. This significantly extends the recommendations by Ehkirch and Matsumae (2024) for measuring intersubjectivity inside co-creative groups, adding a new perspective towards the users.

7.3.1.3 Feedback-Resistance Effect

Several studies in this thesis provided contributions to the theoretical discussion on learning from feedback. Most of the findings confirm researchers who found that feedback does not induce learning (Kruger & Dunning, 1999; Pallier et al., 2002; Schlösser et al., 2013), which means that intersubjectivity can be seen as a static trait. Besides confirming existing theory, there were previously unknown results, such as the dimension of understandability as a key dimension for the movement of co-creators' self-assessments. The most extraordinary contribution to the theory may be the feedback-resistance effect. As a hitherto unknown phenomenon, it describes an effect where co-creators increase their self-assessment and show irrational behavior after receiving feedback.

7.3.1.4 Intersubjectivity as a Selection Criterion for Co-Creators

Since it could be assumed that intersubjectivity cannot be learned or can only be learned with great effort and time, it is advisable to include intersubjectivity in the list of selection criteria for innovation co-creation projects where the use of ideas by others is intended. Previous research has intensively discussed suitable skills and stages for co-creating (P. Berthon et al., 2011; Hoffman et al., 2010; Kristensson et al., 2004; Oßwald et al., 2019; T. Schweisfurth, 2016; T. G. Schweisfurth & Herstatt, 2015; Schweitzer et al., 2014; von Hippel, 1986). Considering intersubjectivity as an essential co-creation trait beyond expertise like market or technical knowledge might add a new overarching dimension to the selection of co-creators. Intersubjectivity is comparatively less difficult to determine during a workshop than other currently discussed skills like innovativeness or creativity (Hoffman et al., 2010), and it may be a new overarching selection criterion. Intersubjectivity could complement the user-knowledge skills of co-creator types such as lead users (Huang et al., 2018; Shih et al., 2010; von Hippel, 1986) or emergent nature co-creators (Hoffman et al., 2010; Vernette & Kidar, 2013).

7.3.2 Implications for Management

Generating market-relevance beyond one individual in open innovation is challenging, as co-creators are biased (Ariely, 2008). Especially if a co-created idea is to be used by people other than the co-creator, intersubjectivity between both is essential. It may be important for managers to know that intersubjectivity is a key skill for stepping beyond individuality. It cannot, however, be effectively achieved by learning through immediate feedback. Even if the theory and a number of practical methods assume learning effects, and this can perhaps be achieved under certain circumstances (Krajc & Ortmann, 2008; Mayo et al., 2012; Mezirow, 1991; Murphy, 2017), learning intersubjectivity may take a long time, require enormous effort, and can sometimes be perceived as an unpleasant experience by co-creators. Whether intersubjectivity is a static trait or a skill that can be learned with effort and time, neither is compatible with the typically rather short-term integration of co-creators in open innovation. A complete learning process would turn a co-creator into a professional designer who may have fewer evaluation biases and may then bring less user knowledge and probably other biases. Rather, managers could focus on intersubjectivity as a fixed trait and proactively work with it. The following sections present a proposal for an intersubjectivity working model. It is a compilation of how innovating organizations and intermediaries could implement the concept of intersubjectivity in innovation co-creation projects with three working options to identify, measure, and balance intersubjectivity.

7.3.2.1 An Intersubjectivity Working Model

The key question for innovating organizations and intermediaries may be how to work with intersubjectivity. A compilation of the empirical findings emerging from this thesis provides three options for how innovating organizations and intermediaries can address intersubjectivity, illustrated in Fig. 7.2: (1) Co-creators with an intersubjective trait can be identified, (2) intersubjectivity can be measured, and (3) it can be balanced with a range of methods.

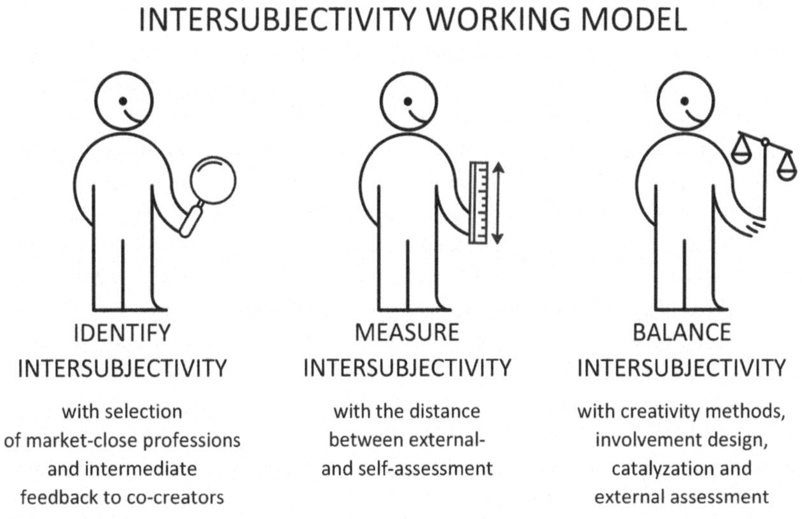

Fig. 7.2 Derived proposal for an intersubjectivity working model. (Author's illustration)

7.3.2.1.1 Identify Intersubjectivity

Before integration, co-creators with intersubjective traits could be selected. These co-creators are found in professions close to the market. They include business developers, innovation consultants, designers, and marketing managers. Already-integrated co-creators, e.g., those in a workshop group, can probably be identified by mutual feedback. Integrating a mutual feedback step about understandability in co-creation workshops helps to gain initial clues about top performers in market relevance beyond the individual using the Dunning-Kruger test (Kruger & Dunning, 1999). In this mutual feedback step, participants give each other anonymous feedback on the understandability of their ideas, e.g., via a voting platform. The results are then divided into quartiles. Ideas from participants in the third quartile were likely to be assessed as the most realistic. The top performers in the fourth quartile were likely to contribute the ideas with the most market potential. This provides the opportunity to discard individually overestimated ideas from the first and second quartile at an early stage and focus on potentially more market-relevant contributions. As Study IV showed, this method of identifying high-performing co-creators works reasonably well with smaller, unrepresentative groups, too.

7.3.2.1.2 Measure Intersubjectivity

In order to determine levels of intersubjectivity and to measure possible changes, it is first necessary to define its direction, i.e., between which roles intersubjectivity is to be established. Once the direction of intersubjectivity is defined, an intersubjective level can be determined as the difference between individual subjective perceptions of the individual roles in the innovation co-creation process, e.g., between a user and a co-creator. Intersubjectivity (P_t) may be determined as the distance between average mutual (or external) assessments (AMA) and self-assessment (SA) at a fixed measure point in time t with the equation $P_t = SA_t - AMA_t$. This approach requires assessments of both roles involved. Assessments can be collected anonymously via voting tools with a minimum of effort. Since co-creators are additionally potential users of the ideas, the determination of intersubjectivity between both roles similarly applies on a smaller scale with mutual feedback among co-creators. This approach requires much less effort than subjecting already co-created ideas to another co-creation process in a later stage, as is often the case today for identifying possible marketing potential beyond the individual co-creator.

In long-term co-designing within a fixed group, intersubjectivity can additionally be measured in a dynamic context with the equation $P(n + 1) = P(n) + \Delta P$ (Ehkirch & Matsumae, 2024). The static data here come from interpersonal factors like subjective feedback, behavior observations, or measurements of bio signals. Interpersonal factors deliver the dynamic data. This model mainly considers the processes among grouped co-creators over a longer period of time; it is not fully suited to measuring intersubjectivity beyond the co-creator group, and it requires additional effort to collect the data.

7.3.2.1.3 Balance Intersubjectivity

This thesis surveyed a plethora of recommendations for balancing methods to achieve intersubjectivity in open innovation and thereby overcome evaluation biases that have a negative impact. These methods can be divided into three categories: creativity methods, involvement design, catalyzation of ideas, and external assessment. The following section and Table 7.2 deliver a summarized overview for practitioners.

Table 7.2 Methods for balancing intersubjectivity

METHODS FOR BALANCING INTERSUBJECTIVITY	
CREATIVITY METHODS	• Design thinking (Plattner et al., 2009) • "Kill your darlings" technique (Plattner et al., 2009) • Confrontation with other perspectives by constant interaction with other users or working in groups • Thinking hats (de Bono, 1990) • Future newspapers • "Explain it to a layperson" technique • Change of location • Time pressure • Design sprints (Knapp, 2016)
INVOLVEMENT DESIGN	• Clear guidelines: Precise formulation of research questions and idea selection criteria (Dahl & Moreau, 2007) • Diversity in workshop groups (Schuurman et al., 2015) • Selection of co-creators
CATALYZATION and EXTERNAL ASSESSMENT	• Idea selection by innovating organization or other experts in the field • Consensual Assessment Technique (Amabile, 1982) • Professional designers as catalysts (Verganti, 2009; Manzini, 2015)

- CREATIVITY METHODS
  Creativity methods help gain intersubjectivity. Design thinking (Plattner et al., 2009), which is inspired by designing processes, is the most preferred method for this. It focuses on users, technological feasibility, and economic viability at early stages. The associated "kill your darlings" technique dismisses favorite ideas to improve critical distance. Constantly interacting with other users and working in groups can change of perspectives. Other methods for this are

"thinking hats" (de Bono, 1990), "future newspapers," simplifying through "explain it to a layperson," and change of location. Time pressure is another promising strategy to avoid evaluation biases. Design sprints (Knapp, 2016), a dense derivation of design thinking achieves results quickly and in a structured way. The sprints help intermediaries prevent perfectionism or destructive group dynamics, involve reluctant co-creators, and decline unpromising concepts.

- INVOLVEMENT DESIGN
  The involvement design can help to establish intersubjectivity. Communication issues regarding a common understanding can be solved by clearer guidelines. Co-creators feel more comfortable in a constrained environment, e.g., through precise formulation of research questions and selection criteria (Dahl & Moreau, 2007), which significantly increases useful ideas. Most realistic co-creation results can be achieved by diversity in workshop groups (Schuurman et al., 2015). A suitable selection of co-creators is crucial to ensure that the composition of the teams is socially and professionally appropriate to the task.
- CATALYZATION OF IDEAS AND EXTERNAL ASSESSMENT
  Catalyzation of ideas and external assessment is one of the most common methods for dealing with subjectivity. It includes selection by the organizer or experts in the field. It could be considered that external assessors can be biased, too (Burcharth et al., 2014), and professional closeness can induce a more critical attitude (Boudreau et al., 2012). Ideas can be externally catalyzed into a consensual solution by experts in the field using the Consensual Assessment Technique (Amabile, 1982). This is particularly suitable for identifying commonalities in individual tacit knowledge—one of the great strengths of open innovation. Professional designers can take the role of catalysts by incorporating collaborative ideas into their work (Manzini, 2015; Verganti, 2009).

7.4 Outlook

This thesis may answer some questions about intersubjectivity in innovation co-creation—at the same time, it opens new doors. The exploratory sequential mixed methods approach used here made it possible, to a certain extent, to balance out the weaknesses of single methods. It enabled in-depth triangulation from qualitative and quantitative studies with experts, in the laboratory, and in different innovation co-creation workshops for a holistic overview (Morse, 1991; Rossman & Wilson, 1985). The results are only a beginning, though, as some topics could not be explored in depth. For example, this thesis focused on the inbound variation of open innovation by integrating external knowledge into organizations (Gassmann & Enkel, 2004). It may be a promising avenue for future research to additionally examine intersubjectivity in outbound or coupled processes, as they imply different roles and conditions. This may broaden the view on intersubjectivity in open innovation even further. There are more aspects that appeared contradictory in the context of this thesis or could not yet be comprehensively researched. These are presented below.

Correlation between intersubjectivity and emergent nature co-creators

Emergent nature co-creators are described as being able to understand the needs of a wider user community early by being imaginative and reflective. They have a high degree of solution information for typical consumer needs (Hoffman et al., 2010; Vernette & Kidar, 2013). This deep understanding of users and the ability for reflection could mean something similar to intersubjectivity, defined as a shared understanding (Burford et al., 2013; Cash et al., 2017; Shapin, 2017; Talamo & Pozzi, 2011), which is based on the ability for critical distance (Chong, 2013). Intersubjectivity is comparatively less difficult to determine during a workshop than other associated skills like innovativeness or creativity (Hoffman et al., 2010) and may be another characteristic of emergent nature co-creators. As this co-creator type is highly sought-after for their market-relevant skills and has not yet been extensively researched, an investigation of a possible correlation between intersubjectivity and emergent nature co-creators may be of great interest. This might be realized by replicating the original laboratory experiment as suggested by Hoffman et al. (2010) in combination with the field quasi-experimental setting from Study IV in this thesis.

Feedback resistance

The need to create and thereby feel empowered is considered as deeply rooted in human beings. This seems logical, given the growth of user innovation movements and their remarkable economic impact (Ogawa & Piller, 2006; Ogawa & Pongtanalert, 2012). This thesis, on the contrary, revealed evidence of co-creators lacking effort. Moreover, a feedback-resistance effect was repeatedly observed in behavior and self-assessment after receiving feedback. One reason might be that learning from feedback cannot be internalized in the short term (Mayo et al., 2012; Mezirow, 1991). Another explanation derived from data was that highly biased co-creators may become self-centered and therefore apathetic, idle, and closed-off. It could likewise be that some co-creators just enjoy the process of co-creating itself and therefore do not care about the results, as described in the one-away effect (Ruan et al., 2024). None of this explains why most of the top performers in intersubjectivity were not likewise deterred by feedback. The reason was that these co-creators believed they were good at assessing the real market potential of their ideas—and they were right. This demonstrates that feedback resistance does not necessarily mean a lack of intersubjectivity.

These different results and reasons for feedback resistance suggest two promising approaches for further research. First, an interesting path might be to confirm the feedback-resistance effect as the 30th evaluation bias. This might be done with another laboratory experiment involving external assessment for controlling "real" market relevance. Secondly, it may be important to know to what extent the co-creators who lack effort are a subgroup with a common reason that may be looked at more closely, or whether it is a phenomenon that has various individual causes. This might be investigated with another experiment.

Transfer of evaluation biases to other users

The empirical part of this thesis showed in several studies that evaluation biases are mostly an individual matter with different impacts. The turning point between positive and negative impacts of evaluation biases was defined as "creating for oneself or for others." It was found that evaluation biases may become problematic in empowerment dimensions other than "by me for one" (Maier & Baccarella, 2024). There are nevertheless two exceptions where the higher valuation of the invested effort is transferred to other users together with the product. This transfer of an evaluation bias would naturally indicate a high degree of intersubjectivity. However, it is unclear how this occurs. The corresponding biases are the handmade effect (Fuchs et al., 2015), which makes self-made products attractive to their users, and the innovation effect of user design (Schreier et al., 2013), where co-created products directly increase consumers' perceptions of the producer's innovative ability. Both biases are located in the co-creator empowerment dimension "by others for many," which is characterized by customers mostly reacting positively to user-designed products (Gebauer et al., 2013). For innovation co-creation, where the use of the idea by others is intended from the outset, it might be crucial to identify the mechanisms that lead to the transferability of positive perceptions to third-party users. Another relevant question would be whether only positive perceptions are transferred, as described in the theory, or whether this similarly applies to negative attitudes towards the creation. This may allow further conclusions on how intersubjectivity is transferred across the different dimensions of co-creator empowerment, adding another facet to the concept of intersubjectivity in open innovation.

7.5 Conclusion

Users legitimately insist on their individual right to be designers of the things they use. Objectively, an IKEA bookshelf is not lovelier because it was built by users with love. Self-made things are more likely to be imperfect, making them all the more loveable because they are more individual. This leading-to-love in the sense of the IKEA effect is what makes co-creation so special. The ability to identify with being a designer, even if only in theory, is enormously meaningful to people. Certainly, evaluation biases generate some "misunderstood artists". As long as this happens solely on an individual level, everyone benefits.

Once other users are involved, these benefits can turn into risks for efficient innovation processes. In open innovation, Joseph Beuys' introductory quote may be adapted as follows: "*Every user is a co-creator—but not every user is an intersubjective co-creator.*" Every co-creator has a similarly high opinion of themselves as a designer, only their individual intersubjectivity towards others changes. The challenge is to identify the professional, i.e., intersubjective co-creators. This finding is reflected in the Dunning-Kruger effect, which built the basis for the two field experiments in this thesis. This insight may likewise enable future identification of intersubjective co-creators in workshops through mutual feedback.

For bridging the former gap between designers and users, more concepts can be taken from design to open innovation than the "thinking": intersubjectivity in open innovation is certainly there, it just has not been visible enough up to now. This thesis demonstrates that intersubjectivity has many different connections to innovation co-creation. It may establish intersubjectivity between different disciplines such as open innovation, design, and behavioral economics. Hopefully, this thesis will contribute to a more comprehensive picture and further research on intersubjectivity in open innovation.

Finally, it remains to be said that not only labor leads to love, as the subtitle of the IKEA effect suggests: **co-creation leads to love**, too.

"

Do you think the same?

References

Abdullah, R., & Hübner, R. (2005). *Piktogramme und Icons: Pflicht oder Kür?* (1. Auflage). Schmidt Hermann Verlag. https://books.google.de/books?id=vL4ZngEACAAJ

Alam, I. (2002). An exploratory investigation of user involvement in new service development. *Journal of the Academy of Marketing Science, 30*, 250–261. https://doi.org/10.1177/0092070302303006

Alicke, M., & Govorun, O. (2005). The better-than-average effect. In M. Alicke, D. Dunning, & J. Kruger (Eds.), *The self in social judgement* (pp. 83–106). Psychology Press.

Amabile, T. M. (1982). Social psychology of creativity: A consensual assessment technique. *Journal of Personality and Social Psychology, 43*(5), 997–1013. https://doi.org/10.1037/0022-3514.43.5.997

Amabile, T. M. (1983). The social psychology of creativity: A componential conceptualization. *Journal of Personality and Social Psychology, 45*(2), 357–376. https://doi.org/10.1037/0022-3514.45.2.357

Ariely, D. (2008). *Predictably irrational.* HarperCollins.

Arkes, H. R., & Blumer, C. (1985). The psychology of sunk cost. *Organizational Behavior and Human Decision Processes, 35*(1), 124–140. https://doi.org/10.1016/0749-5978(85)90049-4

Aronson, E., & Mills, J. (1959). The effect of severity of initiation on liking for a group. *The Journal of Abnormal and Social Psychology.* https://doi.org/10.1037/h0047195

Atakan, S. S., Bagozzi, R. P., & Yoon, C. (2014). Consumer participation in the design and realization stages of production: how self-production shapes consumer evaluations and relationships to products. *International Journal of Research in Marketing*. https://doi.org/10.1016/j.ijresmar.2014.05.003

Bandura, A. (1977). Self-efficacy: toward a unifying theory of behavioral change. *Psychological Review*. https://doi.org/10.1037/0033-295x.84.2.191

Batey, M. (2012). The measurement of creativity: from definitional consensus to the introduction of a new heuristic framework. *Creativity Research Journal, 24*(1), 55–65. https://doi.org/10.1080/10400419.2012.649181

Baumeister, R. F., & Leary, M. R. (1997). Writing narrative literature reviews. *Review of General Psychology, 1*(3), 311–320. https://doi.org/10.1037/1089-2680.1.3.311

M. Oßwald, *When Co-Creation Leads to Love*, Markt- und Unternehmensentwicklung Markets and Organisations,
https://doi.org/10.1007/978-3-658-48890-1

Berthon, P., Campbell, C., Pitt, L., & McCarthy, I. (2011). Creative consumers: awareness, attitude and action. *Journal of Consumer Marketing*, *28*(7), 500–507. https://doi.org/10.1108/07363761111181482

Berthon, P. R., Pitt, L. F., McCarthy, I., & Kates, S. M. (2007). When customers get clever: managerial approaches to dealing with creative consumers. *Business Horizons*, *50*(1), 39–47. https://doi.org/10.1016/j.bushor.2006.05.005

Bessant, J., & Rush, H. (1995). Building bridges for innovation: the role of consultants in technology transfer. *Research Policy*, *24*(1), 97–114. https://doi.org/10.1016/0048-7333(93)00751-E

Beuys, J. (2002). *Sprechen über Deutschland: Rede, gehalten am 20. November 1985 in den Münchner Kammerspielen*. FIU.

Bissola, R., Imperatori, B., & Colonel, R. T. (2014). Enhancing the creative performance of new product teams: an organizational configurational approach. *Journal of Product Innovation Management*, 31(2), 375–391. https://doi.org/10.1111/jpim.12101

Biyalogorsky, E., Boulding, W., & Staelin, R. (2006). Stuck in the past: why managers persist with new product failures. *Journal of Marketing*. https://doi.org/10.1509/jmkg.70.2.108

Bogers, M., Zobel, A. K., Afuah, A., Almirall, E., Brunswicker, S., Dahlander, L., Frederiksen, L., Gawer, A., Gruber, M., Haefliger, S., Hagedoorn, J., Hilgers, D., Laursen, K., Magnusson, M. G., Majchrzak, A., McCarthy, I. P., Moeslein, K. M., Nambisan, S., Piller, F. T., … Ter Wal, A. L. J. (2017). The open innovation research landscape: established perspectives and emerging themes across different levels of analysis. *Industry and Innovation*, 24(1), 8–40. https://doi.org/10.1080/13662716.2016.1240068

Boudreau, K. J., Guinan, E., Lakhani, K. R., & Riedl, C. (2012). The novelty paradox & bias for normal science: evidence from randomized medical grant proposal evaluations. *SSRN Electronic Journal*. https://doi.org/10.2139/ssrn.2184791

Brunneder, J., & Dholakia, U. (2018). The self-creation effect: making a product supports its mindful consumption and the consumer's well-being. *Marketing Letters*, *29*(3), 377–389. https://doi.org/10.1007/s11002-018-9465-6

Bryman, A., & Bell, E. (2011). *Business Research Methods* (3rd ed.). Oxford University Press.

Bühren, C., & Pleßner, M. (2014). The trophy effect. *Journal of Behavioral Decision Making*. https://doi.org/10.1002/bdm.1812

Burcharth, A. L. D. A., Knudsen, M. P., & Søndergaard, H. A. (2014). Neither invented nor shared here: the impact and management of attitudes for the adoption of open innovation practices. *Technovation*, 34(3), 149–161. https://doi.org/10.1016/j.technovation.2013.11.007

Burford, G., Hoover, E., Velasco, I., Janoušková, S., Jimenez, A., Piggot, G., Podger, D., & Harder, M. K. (2013). Bringing the "missing pillar" into sustainable development goals: towards intersubjective values-based indicators. *Sustainability (Switzerland)*. https://doi.org/10.3390/su5073035

Campbell, D. T., & Stanley, J. L. (1966). *Experimental and quasi-experimental designs for research*. Rand McNally.

Cash, P., Dekoninck, E. A., & Ahmed-Kristensen, S. (2017). Supporting the development of shared understanding in distributed design teams. *Journal of Engineering Design*, *28*(3), 147–170. https://doi.org/10.1080/09544828.2016.1274719

Cassar, A., & Friedman, D. (2004). *Economics lab.* Routledge. https://doi.org/10.4324/978 0203356845

Chen, D. T. V., Wang, Y. M., & Lee, W. C. (2016). Challenges confronting beginning researchers in conducting literature reviews. *Studies in Continuing Education, 38*(1), 47–60. https://doi.org/10.1080/0158037X.2015.1030335

Cherryholmes, C. H. (1992). Notes on pragmatism and scientific realism. *Educational Researcher, 21*(6), 13. https://doi.org/10.2307/1176502

Chesbrough, H. W. (2003). The era of open innovation. *MIT Sloan Management Review.*

Chesbrough, H. W. (2011). Open services innovation: rethinking your business to grow and compete in a new era. In *Business.* https://doi.org/10.1017/CBO9781107415324.004

Chong, P. (2013). Legitimate judgment in art, the scientific world reversed? Maintaining critical distance in evaluation. *Social Studies of Science.* https://doi.org/10.1177/030631271 2475256

Cooper-White, P. (2014). *Intersubjectivity BT—Encyclopedia of Psychology and Religion* (D. A. Leeming, Ed.; pp. 882–886). Springer US. https://doi.org/10.1007/978-1-4614-6086-2_9182

Creswell, J. W., & Creswell, J. D. (2018). *Research Design: Qualitative, Quantitative, and Mixed Methods Approaches* (5th ed.). SAGE Publications.

Creswell, J. W., & Poth, C. N. (2016). *Qualitative inquiry and research design: choosing among five approaches.* Sage Publications, Incorporated.

Cui, A. S., & Wu, F. (2015). Utilizing customer knowledge in innovation: antecedents and impact of customer involvement on new product performance. *Journal of the Academy of Marketing Science.* https://doi.org/10.1007/s11747-015-0433-x

Dahl, D. W., & Moreau, C. P. (2007). Thinking inside the box: why consumers enjoy constrained creative experiences. *Journal of Marketing Research, 44*(3), 357–369. https://doi.org/10.1509/jmkr.44.3.357

D'Angelo, J., Diehl, K., & Cavanaugh, L. (2019). Lead by example? Custom-made examples created by close others lead consumers to make dissimilar choices. *Journal of Consumer Research, 46*, 750–773. https://doi.org/10.1093/jcr/ucz019

de Bono, E. (1990). *Six thinking hats.* Penguin Books.

Dittmar, H. (1993). The social psychology of material possessions. To have is to be. *Environmental Psychology.* https://doi.org/10.1016/0167-4870(93)90011-9

Dunning, D. (2011). The Dunning-Kruger effect. On being ignorant of one's own ignorance. In *Advances in Experimental Social Psychology* (Vol. 44). https://doi.org/10.1016/B978-0-12-385522-0.00005-6

Dykstra, H., O'Flaherty, S., & Whillans, A. V. (2023). The buy-in effect: when increasing initial effort motivates behavioral follow-through. *Harvard Business School.*

Ehkirch, Q., & Matsumae, A. (2024). Understanding the influence of interpersonal factors on interactions in co-design through intersubjectivity: A systematic literature review. *Design Science, 10*, 1–29. https://doi.org/10.1017/dsj.2024.1

Ehrlinger, J., & Dunning, D. (2003). How chronic self-views influence (and potentially mislead) estimates of performance. *Journal of Personality and Social Psychology, 84*(1), 5–17. https://doi.org/10.1037/0022-3514.84.1.5

Elmquist, M., Fredberg, T., & Ollila, S. (2009). Exploring the field of open innovation. *European Journal of Innovation Management, 12*(3), 326–345. https://doi.org/10.1108/146010 60910974219

Ermen, R. (2010). *Joseph Beuys* (2. Auflage). Rowohlt.

Fischbacher, U. (2007). z-Tree: Zurich toolbox for ready-made economic experiments. *Experimental Economics*, *10*(2), 171–178. https://doi.org/10.1007/s10683-006-9159-4

Fisher, R. J. (1993). Social desirability bias and the validity of indirect questioning. *Journal of Consumer Research*, *20*(2), 303. https://doi.org/10.1086/209351

Fleischer, J. (2004, September). The IKEA effect. *InFurniture*, *5*(11), 25–32.

Fombelle, P., Bone, S., & Lemon, K. (2016). Responding to the 98%: face-enhancing strategies for dealing with rejected customer ideas. *Journal of the Academy of Marketing Science*, *44*. https://doi.org/10.1007/s11747-015-0469-y

Franke, N., Keinz, P., & Steger, C. J. (2009). Testing the value of customization: When do customers really prefer products tailored to their preferences? *Journal of Marketing*, *73*(5), 103–121. https://doi.org/10.1509/jmkg.73.5.103

Franke, N., Poetz, M. K., & Schreier, M. (2014). Integrating problem solvers from analogous markets in new product ideation. *Management Science*. https://doi.org/10.1287/mnsc.2013.1805

Franke, N., & Schreier, M. (2010). Why customers value self-designed products: the importance of process effort and enjoyment. *Journal of Product Innovation Management*. https://doi.org/10.1111/j.1540-5885.2010.00768.x

Franke, N., Schreier, M., & Kaiser, U. (2010). The "I designed it myself" effect in mass customization. *Management Science*, *56*(1), 125–140. https://doi.org/10.1287/mnsc.1090.1077

Fuchs, C., Prandelli, E., & Schreier, M. (2010). The psychological effects of empowerment strategies on consumers' product demand. *Journal of Marketing*, *74*(1), 65–79. https://doi.org/10.1509/jmkg.74.1.65

Fuchs, C., Schreier, M., & van Osselaer, S. M. J. (2015). The handmade effect: what's love got to do with it? *Journal of Marketing*. https://doi.org/10.1509/jm.14.0018

Furby, L. (1991). Understanding the psychology of possession and ownership: a personal memoir and an appraisal of our progress. *Journal of Social Behavior & Personality*, *6*(6), 457–463. https://doi.org/10.1017/CBO9781107415324.004

Galison, P. (1998). Judgment against objectivity. In *Picturing Science, Producing Art*. Routledge.

Gassmann, O., & Enkel, E. (2004). Towards a theory of open innovation: three core process archetypes. *University of St. Gallen*.

Gebauer, J., Füller, J., & Pezzei, R. (2013). The dark and the bright side of co-creation: triggers of member behavior in online innovation communities. *Journal of Business Research*, *66*(9), 1516–1527. https://doi.org/10.1016/j.jbusres.2012.09.013.

Gioia, D. A., Corley, K. G., & Hamilton, A. L. (2013). Seeking qualitative rigor in inductive research: notes on the Gioia Methodology. *Organizational Research Methods*, *16*(1), 15–31. https://doi.org/10.1177/1094428112452151

Gordon, M. E., Slade, L. A., & Schmitt, N. (1986). The "science of the sophomore" revisited: from conjecture to empiricism. *Academy of Management Review*. https://doi.org/10.5465/amr.1986.4282666

Grant, A. M., & Wall, T. D. (2009). The neglected science and art of quasi-experimentation. *Organizational Research Methods*. https://doi.org/10.1177/1094428108320737

Greiner, B. (2015). Subject pool recruitment procedures: organizing experiments with ORSEE. *Journal of the Economic Science Association*, 1(1), 114–125. https://doi.org/10.1007/s40881-015-0004-4

Greve, K., Martinez, V., Jonas, J., Neely, A., & Moeslein, K. (2016). *Facilitating co-creation in living labs: the JOSEPHS study*. Cambridge University Institute for Manufacturing.

Haller, J. B. A., Velamuri, V. K., Schneckenberg, D., & Möslein, K. M. (2017). Exploring the design elements of open evaluation. *Journal of Strategy and Management*, 10(1), 40–65. https://doi.org/10.1108/JSMA-05-2015-0039

Hammersley, M. (2013). *What is qualitative research?* Continuum/Bloomsbury.

Hirschmann, A. O. (1970). *exit, voice, and loyalty responses to decline in firms, organizations, and states*. Harvard University Press.

Ho, D. K., Ma, J., & Lee, Y. (2011). Empathy @ design research: a phenomenological study on young people experiencing participatory design for social inclusion. *CoDesign*, 7(2), 95–106. https://doi.org/10.1080/15710882.2011.609893

Hocevar, D. (1980). Intelligence, divergent thinking, and creativity. *Intelligence*, 4(1), 25–40. https://doi.org/10.1016/0160-2896(80)90004-5

Hoffman, D. L., Kopalle, P. K., & Novak, T. P. (2010). The “right” consumers for better concepts: identifying consumers high in emergent nature to develop new product concepts. *Journal of Marketing Research*, *47*(5), 854–865. https://doi.org/10.1509/jmkr.47.5.854

Huang, P., Tafti, A., & Mithas, S. (2018). Platform sponsor investments and user contributions in knowledge communities: the role of knowledge seeding. *MIS Quarterly*, *42*(1), 213–240. https://doi.org/10.25300/MISQ/2018/13490

Hubert, A. (2005). Laura Shapiro, something from the oven: reinventing dinner in 1950s america. *Anthropology of Food*, *4*. https://doi.org/10.4000/aof.233

Husserl, E. (1931). *Meditations Cartesiennes: Introduction à la phenomenologie*. Armand Collin.

Ishiyama, F. I., & Munson, P. A. (1993). Development and validation of a self-critical cognition scale. *Psychological Reports*, 72(1), 147–154. https://doi.org/10.2466/pr0.1993.72.1.147

Juntunen, M., & Lehenkari, M. (2021). A narrative literature review process for an academic business research thesis. *Studies in Higher Education*, *46*(2), 330–342. https://doi.org/10.1080/03075079.2019.1630813

Kahneman, D., Knetsch, J. L., & Thaler, R. H. (1991). Anomalies: the endowment effect, loss aversion, and status quo bias. *Journal of Economic Perspectives*. https://doi.org/10.1257/jep.5.1.193

Kahnemann, D., Knetsch, J. L., & Thaler, R. H. (1990). Experimental tests of the endowment effect and the coase theorem. *Journal of Political Economy*.

Kaiser, U., Schreier, M., & Janiszewski, C. (2016). The self-expressive customization of a product can improve your performance. *Journal of Marketing Research*, *54*. https://doi.org/10.1509/jmr.14.0293

Katz, D., & Kahn, R. L. (1966). *The social psychology of organizations*. Wiley.

Katz, R., & Allen, T. J. (1982). Investigating the not invented here (NIH) syndrome: a look at the performance, tenure, and communication patterns of 50 R&D project groups. *R&D Management*, *12*(1), 7–20. https://doi.org/10.1111/j.1467-9310.1982.tb00478.x

Katzy, B., Turgut, E., Holzmann, T., & Sailer, K. (2013). Innovation intermediaries: a process view on open innovation coordination. *Technology Analysis & Strategic Management, 25*(3), 295–309. https://doi.org/10.1080/09537325.2013.764982

Kayser, E. (2009). Lessons learned from retail—capturing the IKEA effect. *2009 13th International Conference on Intelligence in Next Generation Networks*, 1–8. https://doi.org/10.1109/ICIN.2009.5357073

Knapp, J. (2016). *Sprint: How to solve big problems and test new ideas in just five days*. Simon & Schuster Paperbacks.

Krajc, M., & Ortmann, A. (2008). Are the unskilled really that unaware? An alternative explanation. *Journal of Economic Psychology, 29*(5), 724–738. https://doi.org/10.1016/j.joep.2007.12.006

Krämer, K. C. (2015). *What's mine, is yours? Exploring the diffusion of co-creation expertise in organizations* [Dissertation]. Friedrich-Alexander-Universität Erlangen-Nürnberg.

Kristensson, P., Gustafsson, A., & Archer, T. (2004). Harnessing the creative potential among users. *Journal of Product Innovation Management, 21*, 4–14. https://doi.org/10.1111/j.0737-6782.2004.00050.x

Kristensson, P., Matthing, J., & Johansson, N. (2008). Key strategies for the successful involvement of customers in the co-creation of new technology-based services. *International Journal of Service Industry Management*. https://doi.org/10.1108/09564230810891914

Kruger, J., & Dunning, D. (1999). Unskilled and unaware of it: how difficulties in recognizing one's own incompetence lead to inflated self-assessments. *Journal of Personality and Social Psychology, 77*(6), 1121–1134. https://doi.org/10.1037/0022-3514.77.6.1121

Kruger, J., & Gilovich, T. (2004). Actions, intentions, and self-assessment: the road to self-enhancement is paved with good intentions. *Personality and Social Psychology Bulletin, 30*(3), 328–339. https://doi.org/10.1177/0146167203259932

Langley, A., Smallman, C., Tsoukas, H., & Van de Ven, A. H. (2013). process studies of change in organization and management: unveiling temporality, activity, and flow. *Academy of Management Journal, 56*(1), 1–13. https://doi.org/10.5465/amj.2013.4001

Leigh Star, S. (2010). This is not a boundary object: reflections on the origin of a concept. *Science, Technology, & Human Values, 35*(5), 601–617. https://doi.org/10.1177/0162243910377624

Leonard, H., Belk, R. W., & Scammon, D. (2003). Helping others, creating yourself: understanding volunteer vacations. *European Advances in Consumer Research, 6*.

Luchs, M. G., Naylor, R. W., Irwin, J. R., & Raghunathan, R. (2010). The sustainability liability: potential negative effects of ethicality on product preference. *Journal of Marketing, 74*(5), 18–31. https://doi.org/10.1509/jmkg.74.5.18

MacCoun, R. (2003). Experimental and quasi-experimental designs for generalized causal inference, by William R. Shadish, Thomas D. Cook, and Donald T. Campbell. Boston: Houghton Mifflin, 2001, 623 pp. *Journal of Policy Analysis and Management, 22*(2), 330–332. https://doi.org/10.1002/pam.10129

Maier, L., & Baccarella, C. V. (2024). The psychological and behavioral consequences of customer empowerment in new product development: situational framework, review, and research agenda. *Journal of Product Innovation Management, January*, 1–33. https://doi.org/10.1111/jpim.12734

Manzini, E. (2015). *Design, when everybody designs—an introduction to design for social innovation*. The MIT Press.

Marsh, L. E., Kanngiesser, P., & Hood, B. (2018). When and how does labour lead to love? The ontogeny and mechanisms of the IKEA effect. *Cognition*. https://doi.org/10.1016/j.cognition.2017.10.012

Matsumae, A., & Nagai, Y. (2018). The function of co-creation in dynamic mechanism of intersubjectivity formation among individuals. *Proceedings of International Design Conference, DESIGN, 4*, 1925–1936. https://doi.org/10.21278/idc.2018.0141

Mayo, M. (2016). The gender gap in feedback and self-perception. *Harvard Business Review*.

Mayo, M., Kakarika, M., Pastor, J. C., & Brutus, S. (2012). Aligning or inflating your leadership self-image? A longitudinal study of responses to peer feedback in MBA teams. *Academy of Management Learning and Education, 11*(4), 631–652. https://doi.org/10.5465/amle.2010.0069

Merton, R. K. (1972). Insiders and outsiders: a chapter in the sociology of knowledge. In *American Journal of Sociology* (Vol. 78, Issue 1, pp. 9–47). https://doi.org/10.1086/225294

Mezirow, J. (1991). *Transformative dimensions of adult learning*. Jossey-Bass. https://doi.org/10.1177/074171369204200309

Miles, M. B., Huberman, A. M., & Saldana, J. (2013). *Qualitative data analysis: a methods sourcebook. Third Edition*. Sage Publications, Incorporated.

Miller, D. T., & Ross, M. (1975). Self-serving biases in the attribution of causality: fact or fiction? *Psychological Bulletin, 82*(2), 213–225. https://doi.org/10.1037/h0076486

Mochon, D., Norton, M. I., & Ariely, D. (2012). Bolstering and restoring feelings of competence via the IKEA effect. *International Journal of Research in Marketing*. https://doi.org/10.1016/j.ijresmar.2012.05.001

Moore, D. A., & Healy, P. J. (2008). The trouble with overconfidence. *Psychological Review*. https://doi.org/10.1037/0033-295X.115.2.502

Moreau, C. P., & Herd, K. B. (2010). To each his own? How comparisons with others influence consumers' evaluations of their self-designed products. *Journal of Consumer Research, 36*(5), 806–819. https://doi.org/10.1086/644612

Moreau, C., Prandelli, E., Schreier, M., & Hieke, S. (2020). Customization in luxury brands: can Valentino get personal? *Journal of Marketing Research, 57*, 002224372094319. https://doi.org/10.1177/0022243720943191

Morrissette, B. R. (2021). *Cognitive bias codex with definitions—an extension of the work of john manoogian*. https://upload.wikimedia.org/wikipedia/commons/c/ce/Cognitive_Bias_Codex_With_Definitions%2C_an_Extension_of_the_work_of_John_Manoogian_by_Brian_Morrissette.jpg

Morse, J. M. (1991). Approaches to qualitative-quantitative methodological triangulation. *Nursing Research, 40*(2), 120–123.

Mortimer, G., Mathmann, F., & Grimmer, L. (2019). The IKEA effect: how we value the fruits of our labour over instant gratification. *Theconversation.com, April*. https://theconversation.com/the-ikea-effect-how-we-value-the-fruits-of-our-labour-over-instant-gratification-113647

Murphy, M. (2017, January). The Dunning-Kruger effect shows why some people think they're great even when their work is terrible. *Forbes Magazine*. https://www.forbes.com/sites/markmurphy/2017/01/24/the-dunning-kruger-effect-shows-why-some-people-think-theyre-great-even-when-their-work-is-terrible/?sh=65ea9bdf5d7c

Nishikawa, H., Schreier, M., & Ogawa, S. (2013). User-generated versus designer-generated products: a performance assessment at Muji. *International Journal of Research in Marketing, 30*(2), 160–167. https://doi.org/10.1016/j.ijresmar.2012.09.002

Norton, M. I., Mochon, D., & Ariely, D. (2012). The IKEA effect: when labor leads to love. *Journal of Consumer Psychology*. https://doi.org/10.1016/j.jcps.2011.08.002

Nyström, A.-G., Leminen, S., Westerlund, M., & Kortelainen, M. (2014). Actor roles and role patterns influencing innovation in living labs. *Industrial Marketing Management, 43*(3), 483–495. https://doi.org/10.1016/j.indmarman.2013.12.016

Ogawa, S., & Piller, F. T. (2006). Reducing the risks of new product development. In *MIT Sloan Management Review*.

Ogawa, S., & Pongtanalert, K. (2012). Visualizing invisible innovation continent: evidence from global consumer innovation surveys. *SSRN Electronic Journal*. https://doi.org/10.2139/ssrn.1876186

O'Quin, K., & Besemer, S. P. (1989). The development, reliability, and validity of the revised creative product semantic scale. *Creativity Research Journal, 2*(4), 267–278. https://doi.org/10.1080/10400418909534323

Oßwald, M., Rass, M., & Jonas, J. (2019). Selecting co-creators for open innovation. *Open Service Lab Notes*.

Pallier, G., Wilkinson, R., Danthiir, V., Kleitman, S., Knezevic, G., Stankov, L., & Roberts, R. D. (2002). The role of individual differences in the accuracy of confidence judgments. *Journal of General Psychology*. https://doi.org/10.1080/00221300209602099

Parker, G., Manicavasagar, V., Crawford, J., Tully, L., & Gladstone, G. (2006). Assessing personality traits associated with depression: the utility of a tiered model. *Psychological Medicine, 36*(8), 1131–1139. https://doi.org/10.1017/S0033291706007562

Patton, M. Q. (2015). *Qualitative research & evaluation methods: integrating theory and practice* (4th ed.). Sage Publications, Incorporated.

Piller, F., Ihl, C., & Vossen, A. (2011). A typology of customer co-creation in the innovation process—introduction: the idea of open innovation. *New Forms of Collaborative Production and Innovation: Economic, Social, Legal and Technical Characteristics and Conditions, 4*, 1–26. https://doi.org/10.2139/ssrn.1732127

Piller, F. T., Ihl, C., & Vossen, A. (2012). A typology of customer co-creation in the innovation process. *SSRN Electronic Journal*. https://doi.org/10.2139/ssrn.1732127

Plattner, H., Meinel, C., & Weinberg, U. (2009). *Design-thinking*. Mi-Fachverlag. https://link.springer.com/content/pdf/10.1007/978-3-642-13757-0.pdf

Prahalad, C. K., & Ramaswamy, V. (2000). Co-opting customer competence. *Harvard Business Review*. https://doi.org/10.1086/250095

Radtke, T., Liszewska, N., Horodyska, K., Boberska, M., Schenkel, K., & Luszczynska, A. (2019). Cooking together: the IKEA effect on family vegetable intake. *British Journal of Health Psychology, 24*(4), 896–912. https://doi.org/10.1111/bjhp.12385

Ramaswamy, V., & Gouillart, F. (2010). Build the co-creative enterprise. *Harvard Business Review, 88*(10), 100–109.

Reichwald, R., & Piller, F. (2009). Interaktive Wertschöpfung in der Produktion: Individualisierung und Mass Customization. In *Interaktive Wertschöpfung*. https://doi.org/10.1007/978-3-8349-9440-0_5

Richins, M. L. (1987). A multivariate analysis of responses to dissatisfaction. *Journal of the Academy of Marketing Science, 15*(3), 24–31. https://doi.org/10.1177/009207038701500303

Rose, A. V., & Rimes, K. A. (2018). Self-criticism self-report measures: systematic review. *Psychology and Psychotherapy: Theory, Research and Practice, 91*(4), 450–489. https://doi.org/10.1111/papt.12171

Rossman, G. B., & Wilson, B. L. (1985). Numbers and words. *Evaluation Review, 9*(5), 627–643. https://doi.org/10.1177/0193841X8500900505

Roth, A., Dumbach, M., Schliffka, B., & Möslein, K. M. (2017). Successful management of diverse corporate innovation communities. *Journal of Strategy and Management, 10*(1), 2–18. https://doi.org/10.1108/JSMA-08-2015-0066

Roth, K., Globocnik, D., Rau, C., & Neyer, A. K. (2020). Living up to the expectations: The effect of design thinking on project success. *Creativity and Innovation Management, 29*(4), 667–684. https://doi.org/10.1111/caim.12408

Rowley, J., & Slack, F. (2004). Conducting a literature review. *Management Research News, 27*(6), 31–39. https://doi.org/10.1108/01409170410784185

Ruan, B., Polman, E., & Tanner, R. J. (2024). The one-away effect: the pursuit of mere completion. *Journal of Consumer Research, 50*(5), 945–961. https://doi.org/10.1093/jcr/ucad030

Schlag, K., & Tremewan, J. (2016). Simple belief elicitation. *SSRN Electronic Journal*. https://doi.org/10.2139/ssrn.2449224

Schlösser, T., Dunning, D., Johnson, K. L., & Kruger, J. (2013). How unaware are the unskilled? Empirical tests of the "signal extraction" counterexplanation for the Dunning-Kruger effect in self-evaluation of performance. *Journal of Economic Psychology, 39*, 85–100. https://doi.org/10.1016/j.joep.2013.07.004

Schmidt, J. B., & Calantone, R. J. (1998). Are really new product development projects harder to shut down? In *Journal of Product Innovation Management*. https://doi.org/10.1016/S0737-6782(97)00074-X

Schreier, M., Fuchs, C., & Dahl, D. W. (2013). The innovation effect of user design: exploring consumers' innovation perceptions of firms selling products designed by users. *Strategic Direction*. https://doi.org/10.1108/sd.2013.05629baa.002

Schuurman, D., Coorevits, L., Logghe, S., Vandenbroucke, K., Georges, A., & Baccarne, B. (2015). Co-creation in living labs: exploring the role of user characteristics on innovation contribution. *International Journal of Services Sciences, 5*(3/4), 199. https://doi.org/10.1504/ijssci.2015.074218

Schweisfurth, T. (2016). Comparing internal and external lead users as sources of innovation. *Research Policy, 46*. https://doi.org/10.1016/j.respol.2016.11.002

Schweisfurth, T. G., & Herstatt, C. (2015). embedded (lead) users as catalysts to product diffusion. *Creativity and Innovation Management, 24*(1), 151–168. https://doi.org/10.1111/caim.12106

Schweitzer, F., Gassmann, O., & Rau, C. (2014). Lessons from ideation: where does user involvement lead us? *Creativity and Innovation Management, 23*(2), 155–167. https://doi.org/10.1111/caim.12058

Selle, G. (1997). *Geschichte des Design in Deutschland*. Campus Verlag.

Shahar, B., Szepsenwol, O., Zilcha-Mano, S., Haim, N., Zamir, O., Levi-Yeshuvi, S., & Levit-Binnun, N. (2015). A wait-list randomized controlled trial of loving-kindness meditation programme for self-criticism. *Clinical Psychology & Psychotherapy*, *22*(4), 346–356. https://doi.org/10.1002/cpp.1893

Shapin, S. (2017). The sciences of subjectivity. In *Hermeneutic Philosophies of Social Science* (pp. 123–141). Walter de Gruyter GmbH. https://doi.org/10.1515/9783110528374-007

Shih, P. C., Hu, H.-Y., & Farn, C. K. (2010). Lead user participation in brand community: the case of Microsoft MVPs. *Int. J. Electron. Bus. Manag.*, *8*, 323–331. https://api.semanticscholar.org/CorpusID:38477040

Shmueli, O., Fink, L., & Pliskin, N. (2012). Over-requirement in software development: an empirical investigation of the IKEA effect. *ECIS 2012—Proceedings of the 20th European Conference on Information Systems.*

Silvia, P. J., Wigert, B., Reiter-Palmon, R., & Kaufman, J. C. (2012). Assessing creativity with self-report scales: a review and empirical evaluation. *Psychology of Aesthetics, Creativity, and the Arts*, *6*(1), 19–34. https://doi.org/10.1037/a0024071

Staw, B. (1981). The escalation of commitment to a course of action. *Academy of Management. The Academy of Management Review (Pre-1986).*

Talamo, A., & Pozzi, S. (2011). The tension between dialogicality and interobjectivity in cooperative activities. *Culture and Psychology*. https://doi.org/10.1177/1354067X11408131

Teddlie, C., & Tashakkori, A. (2009). *Foundations of mixed methods research: integrating quantitative and qualitative approaches in the social and behavioral sciences*. SAGE Publications.

Temple, B., & Young, A. (2004). Qualitative research and translation dilemmas. *Qualitative Research*. https://doi.org/10.1177/1468794104044430

Terhorst, A., Lusher, D., Bolton, D., Elsum, I., & Wang, P. (2018). Tacit knowledge sharing in open innovation projects. *Project Management Journal*, *49*, 5–19. https://doi.org/10.1177/8756972818781628

Thomas, M., & Alluru, J.-R. (2016). The disastrous consequences of the IKEA effect: Apple, Intel and Wang Labs learning the cost of true love. *Strategic Direction*. https://doi.org/10.1108/SD-10-2015-0145

Urban, D. (1995). *Gestaltung von Piktogrammen*. Novum – Bruckmann.

van de Ven, A. H. (1992). Suggestions for studying strategy process: a research note. *Strategic Management Journal*, *13*(S1), 169–188. https://doi.org/10.1002/smj.4250131013

van de Ven, A. H., & Poole, M. S. (1995). Explaining development and change in organizations. *The Academy of Management Review*, *20*(3), 510. https://doi.org/10.2307/258786

Verganti, R. (2009). *Design driven innovation: changing the rules of competition by radically innovating what things mean*. Harvard Business Review Press.

Vernette, E., & Kidar, L. H. (2013). Co-creation with consumers: who has the competence and wants to cooperate? *International Journal of Market Research*, *55*(4), 539–561. https://doi.org/10.2501/IJMR-2013-047

von Hippel, E. (1986). Lead users: a source of novel product concepts. *Management Science*. https://doi.org/10.1287/mnsc.32.7.791

von Hippel, E. (1994). "Sticky information" and the locus of problem solving: implications for innovation. *Management Science*. https://doi.org/10.1287/mnsc.40.4.429

von Hippel, E. (1998). Economics of product development by users: the impact of "sticky" local information. *Management Science*. https://doi.org/10.1287/mnsc.44.5.629

Walasek, L., Rakow, T., & Matthews, W. J. (2017). When does construction enhance product value? Investigating the combined effects of object assembly and ownership on valuation. *Journal of Behavioral Decision Making*. https://doi.org/10.1002/bdm.1931

West, J., & Gallagher, S. (2006). Challenges of open innovation: the paradox of firm investment in open-source software. *R and D Management*, *36*(3), 319–331. https://doi.org/10.1111/j.1467-9310.2006.00436.x

Whittemore, R., & Knafl, K. (2005). The integrative review: updated methodology. *Journal of Advanced Nursing*, *52*(5), 546–553. https://doi.org/10.1111/j.1365-2648.2005.03621.x

Williams, F. E. (1980). *Creativity assessment packet (CAP)*. D.O.K. Publishers. https://books.google.de/books?id=3duPmwEACAAJ

Wilson, M. (2016). When creative consumers go green: understanding consumer upcycling. *Journal of Product & Brand Management*, *25*(4), 394–399. https://doi.org/10.1108/JPBM-09-2015-0972

Xiao, Y., & Watson, M. (2019). Guidance on conducting a systematic literature review. *Journal of Planning Education and Research*, *39*(1), 93–112. https://doi.org/10.1177/0739456X17723971

The manufacturer's authorised representative in the EU is Springer Nature Customer Service Centre GmbH, Europaplatz 3, 69115 Heidelberg, Germany. If you have any concerns regarding our products, please contact ProductSafety@springernature.com

Printed and bound by CPI Group (UK) Ltd, Croydon, CR0 4YY
01/10/2026
02225951-0001